Everyone
Needs

Everyone Needs an Editor

(Some of Us More Than Others)

A Memoir

Larry McCoy

Bristling With Laughs and Outbursts About the News Business

SUNSTONE
PRESS

SANTA FE

Note: The views and opinions expressed in this book do not necessarily represent those of Sunstone Press or its staff.

"Bullshit Is One Word, Performance Review Two" was first published by *Paradigm*, an online magazine, and an early draft of "A Life Spent in What Is Now, All Too Often, a Frivolous Profession" appeared in *Word Riot*, another online magazine. Some chapters, in slightly different forms, have appeared on the author's website, www.larrymccoyonline.com.

Sunstone books may be purchased for educational, business, or sales promotional use. For information please write: Special Markets Department, Sunstone Press, P.O. Box 2321, Santa Fe, New Mexico 87504-2321.

Book and cover design › Vicki Ahl
Body typeface › Book Antiqua
Printed on acid-free paper
∞
eBook 978-1-61139-345-3

Library of Congress Cataloging-in-Publication Data
McCoy, Larry.
    Everyone needs an editor : (some of us more than others) : a memoir / by Larry McCoy.
        pages cm
    "Bristling with laughs and outbursts about the news business."
    Includes bibliographical references and index.
    ISBN 978-1-63293-041-5 (softcover : alk. paper)
    1. McCoy, Larry. 2. Journalists--United States--Biography. 3. Newspaper
editors--United States--Biography. I. Title.
    PN4874.M3625A3 2015
    070.92--dc23
    [B]
                        2014044056

WWW.SUNSTONEPRESS.COM
SUNSTONE PRESS / POST OFFICE BOX 2321 / SANTA FE, NM 87504-2321 /USA
(505) 988-4418 / ORDERS ONLY (800) 243-5644 / FAX (505) 988-1025

For Irene,

For never complaining about the hours and for enduring a never-ending barrage of shoptalk. (And thanks for doing the chapter drawings.)

Contents

Foreword / 9

Acknowledgements / 11

THE WORKING YEARS

NO LONGER WORKING
BUT STILL PICKING NITS

Foreword

I started out wanting to be a disc jockey and was doing fine at a radio station in Bedford, Indiana, until the boss called me in to disclose a universal truth: "sarcasm doesn't go in a small market." I was twenty, a junior in college and knew she was dead wrong. She also suggested that I "put a smile in my voice." Being twenty and a junior in college, I knew that was absolutely unnecessary.

After graduating from Indiana University, I found a full-time job at a station in Anderson, Indiana. There, six days a week, I entertained listeners with my gift for sarcasm while never bothering to put a smile in my voice. After a couple of months, they fired me.

Not knowing what else to do, I moved to Chicago to be near the girl I wanted to marry and, luckily, drifted into the news business where sarcasm was a way of life and anyone who had a smile in his voice lost it after a month on the overnight shift.

I was a newsman for more than forty-five years—UPI in Chicago and New York, ABC Radio in New York, Radio Free Europe in Munich and CBS Radio and Television in New York. I bounced around a lot, working three times for UPI and twice at both RFE and CBS.

Known for an abrasive (some think highly obnoxious) demeanor in a newsroom, I never really left the trenches and was very hands-on as a manager at RFE and CBS. While not comfortable boasting about any accomplishments, the record shows that when I was a supervisor at CBS News, Radio the newsroom won two Peabody Awards: in 1989 for coverage of the turmoil in China that led to the massacre at Tiananmen Square and in 1995 for reporting on the assassination of Israeli Prime Minister Yitzhak Rabin.

At CBS, I called in new desk assistants to make sure they knew that what we did was serious business, and if they didn't pay attention and stay focused someone would yell at them. Me. But I stressed that didn't mean we shouldn't enjoy ourselves. It's hard to beat going all out at your job and having fun at the same time.

One of my employers won't be identified. They once gave me a year-end bonus of cash and stock options for good work, but we grew tired of each other. I'll leave it at that.

Everything in THE WORKING YEARS section of the book really happened, though this is merely my version of it. Some time frames—in the pieces on performance reviews and the magic of radio, for example— have been compressed. Precise dates of a few incidents were tough to pin down because of fading memories, both mine and others.

I had the pleasure of working alongside many talented anchors, editors, reporters, writers and technicians as well as operations managers who made sure the newsroom had the technical help and facilities it needed. The names of some of these people are listed in the Index. Several names have been changed, and in those cases there is no entry in the Index. I've already been mugged once and see no need to repeat the experience.

Acknowledgements

I want to thank Richard Osborne and John Milne, two old pros in broadcasting and journalism, for reading a draft of the manuscript and making many valuable suggestions, both large and small. I'm probably most grateful that neither of them said, "Throw the damn thing away, McCoy, and take up golf."

Thanks also to Kit Borgman, Linda Coombs and Linda Perlman, former editors and producers at CBS News, for reading and editing an early version of the chapters on stringers. What a delightful feeling that must have been, slashing away at the copy of the old boss.

I appreciate all the time journalists and technicians spent responding to emails and refreshing my memory. Frankly, it was a surprise that three or four of them didn't tell me to go straight to hell.

THE WORKING YEARS

1

The First Two Lessons of Journalism

My first day as a journalist began in the supply room at United Press International in Chicago. I was told to clean it up. Talk about a quick start. Right off the bat there was lesson number one on day one: journalism is a dirty business.

Having never been in an around-the-clock newsroom before, I didn't know what to expect at UPI. The couple of news writing courses I took at Indiana University didn't cover how to neatly stack rolls of teletype paper and other supplies in a small, confined space, but after my supply room duty that first day I became part of the cluster of people behind typewriters. I was scared and unready and knew it.

I couldn't type a lick. I was more or less proud of this deficiency until UPI surprised me with a job offer. I had never thought about learning to type because, don't you know, typing was something girls took in high school back in the '50s. My typing, or lack thereof, never came up when I applied at UPI.

Working there wasn't my idea anyway. I set out to be a disc jockey and after graduating from college got a job at WCBC, a radio station in Anderson, Indiana, owned by a Protestant church. The church folks and I were a marvelous fit. They liked everything about me, including my attitude on and off the air and my smoking in the room they provided me at a church college, where smoking was forbidden. They also had their doubts about my taste in music and that of the other two or three disc jockeys. Not wanting to hear what they considered fast music on their station, they made sure that wouldn't happen by putting Scotch tape over many of the cuts on a standard LP album. Anything with Scotch tape on it was bad, too close to boogie-woogie. Couldn't be played on the air.

When they asked me to leave after several weeks, I had no idea what I wanted to do outside of marry Irene Kristoff, the girl I had dated in college, so I moved to Chicago where she was working. I had no income and no prospects until Irene's boss in the publicity department at WBKB, an ABC Television station, suggested I try the wire services. I did as I was told and UPI bit. The beautiful part of it was that I was going to be paid $76.25 a week, a spectacular $1.25 more than Irene was making. Did I show her or what?

Time has graciously erased much of my memory about my first couple of weeks at UPI. I do remember though being intrigued by the looks and talent of Jesse Bogue, a manager who always seemed to be at his desk regardless of what shift I was on. Jesse was twice as tall as Eddie Arcaro, the jockey, weighed half as much and had the smallest head I've ever seen. Toward the end of his day, he liked to shove a big cigar into his mouth and puff away. It looked like someone had crammed a telephone pole into a cupcake.

Now that I've ridiculed him, let me say that Jesse was a terrific wire service deskman. Knew news, knew politics, knew geography and knew that speed as well as something called accuracy was important. And what really got my attention, he could type like a son of a bitch, like a machine gun. Bam, bam, bambambam, bam, bambambam, bam. Done! Who the hell clued him in that guys typed too?

My approach to coaxing typewriter keys to make an impression on paper was several steps slower than the hunt-and-peck method. My style was search and destroy. I searched and searched the keyboard and then when I spotted the key I wanted I pounded the shit out of it. Or the one next to it.

I got away with this without anyone saying anything until the day the sports editor, Ed Sainsbury, called from either Comiskey Park or Wrigley Field, and I was asked to take dictation of a baseball box score. Ed was a man in a hurry. Hell, he had four kids or more, so he probably lived amid chaos all the time at home and had to talk a mile a minute to be heard and to keep things halfway under control. (As an aside, Ed once took a dare from one of his kids, or maybe the whole brood, and dyed his salt and pepper hair the color of cordovan wingtip shoes. I had a pair of those dreadful things and, after Ed's dye job, could never put them on without thinking of him.)

Anyway, when Ed called with the box score, I was told to take it, and the second I picked up the phone he sprayed names and statistics all over me. This was true journalism, and Kid McCoy clearly wasn't up to it. Not only couldn't I type, I had no idea a typewriter could be set, by a competent operator, to make nice straight columns of numbers. Ed was going so fast and refused to slow down (he may have wanted to race home to start another baby) I began making up abbreviations for players' names, figuring I could sort all this out when Ed finally finished. Smart, huh? Talk about feeling lost and humbled.

At some point Bogue or another person of authority, sensing I might be in over my head, came to look over my shoulder at what I had on paper. All I remember hearing is one word: "Jesus!" So lesson number two was that journalism, at times, could be a religious experience.

I don't know which team was home that day. I sure hope it wasn't the White Sox where Ted Kluszewski was finishing out his career. Big Klu wound up with a .298 lifetime batting average, and I'd hate to think that his numbers might have been good enough to squeeze him into the Hall of Fame if I hadn't mangled the box score that day.

Sorry, Klu.

The Kid Gets Transferred

Soon after this display of incompetence and panic, I was asked if I would like to do something else. No, not mop the newsroom floor, but move to the other side of the room where box scores and stories weren't phoned in by impatient reporters with hair the color of cordovan wingtips. After all, I was told, you have a degree in Radio and Television so maybe the National Radio Wire "is the place for you."

It truly was much more exciting on the radio side of things. You handled major news from all over the world rather than mostly secondary stories from the Midwest. The National Radio staff took UPI copy intended for newspapers and rewrote it into broadcast style for use at radio and television stations. This meant you usually put the source at the front of the lead sentence not at the end as newspapers do and wrote shorter sentences and obviously shorter stories.

I'll never forget the morning National Radio moved a FLASH on Yuri Gagarin's ride into space. The Russians were the first to do it! Good God. You could feel a tingle in the newsroom that morning. Adding to the challenge was something called the Bouverie wire, named after a street in London where UPI had its offices. That wire gave the radio desk access to foreign news being filed into the London bureau before it made its way onto the main U.S. newspaper wire, the A wire. It was great fun to see if you could get a breaking news item on the radio wire before it "hit" the A wire.

The best thing about this new position was all the good writers who—and this was something entirely new to me—talked about writing. If a reporter at UPI or the *Chicago Sun Times* had come up with a well-written, catchy lead, someone on National Radio would notice it and mention it. Mike Royko was beginning to make a name for himself at the *Chicago Daily News*—UPI was in the *Daily News* building on the Chicago River—and a common question around radio was, "Did you read Royko today?" And there were frequent conversations about the people and policies Walter Lippmann and Scotty Reston were zeroing in on in their columns.

Then there were the fascinating observations and revelations about another topic the Kid knew next to nothing about—dicks. Vaughn Packard, one of the radio wire's top commanders, stood in plain sight in the newsroom and, regardless of whether women were or were not present, played with himself. Yes, down there. He rolled the end of his pecker through his pants, using his thumb and the index finger on his right hand. I don't think he realized he was doing this, but he did it almost constantly when he was standing, even at parties while talking to three or four wives of staffers. He had served in the military and perhaps that's what you do in between deployments. Is pecker rolling part of U.S. military manuals, maybe in a chapter on knot tying?

Vaughn was one of several journalists UPI transferred from New York to Chicago when the National Radio desk moved there. The company also brought in a few UPI Lifers who were considered dead-wood after being entrenched in other bureaus for years, stubbornly resisting pleas for change.

Among those unfairly relegated to this category was Ron Dewey. He must have been in his early 40s and, being nearly twice my age, that made him seem old to me. It was Ron who one day, when the conversation had turned to dicks as it frequently did in the good old days of journalism, revealed that some older men have trouble maintaining an erection.

Now this was news! I had never heard such a thing. I wanted to ask, "You mean you can't even use it to type with?" What was the world coming to? First the Russians kick our ass and beat us into space, and now I'm hearing that after a certain age your pecker stops pecking. The guys in high school back in Frankfort, Indiana, were right. You do only have so much of that stuff, and when it's gone that's all there is.

What a lousy situation this is. Or was. Dewey—a straight shooter, so to speak—passed on this frightening information light years before Viagra. While I may have been the only one to whom this was breaking news, to Ron's credit as well as UPI's National Radio desk, he was first with it and he got it right. It doesn't get any better than that in the wire service business.

2

Goodbye, Sun. Hello, Moon.

Not long after my move to the National Radio desk, I was introduced to Thermos World, the glorious midnight to eight a.m. shift, where you're constantly searching for something warm and soothing to keep you going. Some long-timers felt the secret was to bring in two Thermoses, one with soup, the other with coffee. The Kid became a one Thermos guy. Campbell's soup was my constant wee hours friend along with an olive loaf sandwich most mornings and tepid, brown water that came out of a machine, cost a dime, and was allegedly coffee. (I suppose it's too late to sue the vending company for consumer fraud.)

Here I was twenty-two years old, staying up all night to work in the hot shot profession of news, eating lunch at three-thirty a.m. with a candy bar or two at six a.m., aching and sore from my cowlick to my toes, feeling as though I had been hit behind the knees with a baseball bat, and working Saturdays and Sundays plus every holiday. I had, in a word, arrived!

Once a Thermos World shift ended, I did what many normal human beings do after work—I had a drink. There's nothing like a boilermaker (for the beverage-impaired that's a shot of whiskey and a beer) at eight-twenty in the morning. I didn't have many drinking companions at that hour in a bar on Madison Street near the office, although the place did a steady carryout business—guys in ties who came in for their daily (or maybe just the morning) half pint, quickly hidden in their clothing or briefcase.

Many mornings the only person in the bar I knew was a fellow UPIer, Toledo Jack Sizemore, a dapper white-haired hack who had never made a penny off his one true talent, killing flies. The United Nations should have coaxed him out of Thermos World and channeled his expertise to help Third World countries.

I never saw Toledo Jack miss. A fly would only buzz once around his drink before he slapped it flat dead on the bar. "They fly backwards," I seem to remember Toledo Jack saying. "Aim behind them and you'll get them every time." He did and did. I thought I did but didn't. I never could figure out why. Looking back, Toledo Jack was an accomplished multitasker—killing both flies and brain cells and doing it before the banks opened.

Howard was Toledo Jack's first name but at some point there was another Howard Sizemore with more seniority at UPI, so my drinking pal went by a nickname he had picked up while working in Toledo. He wasn't much on imagination with the exception of speculation about possible sexual positions, many of them clearly impossible ones, but he took instructions well and could turn out a decent story if you told him what you thought the lead should be. He also pretended that his skill set didn't include a sense of direction. Nearly every morning that we were out together, he would suggest, "Drop me off on your way home." He lived on the north side of Chicago while I lived south of the city, in Whiting, Indiana. He was good company and usually got a ride.

While Toledo Jack dressed better than any man I ever saw on the overnight (he almost always wore a tie and jacket), he had the pasty look of a Thermos World denizen, someone who didn't get out in the sun enough, if at all. He said he didn't mind the hours, the favorite refrain of

Thermos World volunteers, a breed that believed the lousy hours were the trade-off for not having to see much of the TOMs—the Turkeys Of Management—who generally came in after the sun was up and who frequently said stupid things and made even stupider suggestions.

"It builds character," I have always told youngsters about to be thrown onto the overnight for the first time. That it does, and it's also inhabited by folks you'll never forget. For example, Billy Ferguson (his real name). Billy loved sports and was born in Indiana but, after spending some time with UPI in Atlanta, decided to ignore his Hoosier roots and boasted that he was "one hundred and eighty pounds of All-South." It was more like one hundred and ninety pounds of All-South but that's getting picky.

Billy had a house full of young kids, and at least once a night he would reach into his pockets, hoping to find ten pennies to exchange for a dime for the coffee machine. During his penny search, he would pull out a baby sock or a toy truck, presumably picked up from the floor at home.

Not getting much sleep there, Billy tried to make up for it at the office. During his lunch hour, he would lay down on a desk in the back of the newsroom, and it was my job, as the junior person on duty, to wake him up. He was hard to rouse, and, since these were the days when guys didn't touch each other, my solution was to drop a large wastebasket on the floor near his head. Billy never told me to stop with the dropping of the wastebasket. Perhaps it reminded him of home where he had to deal with infants constantly.

The lunch hour nap was not his only one of the night just his longest. Billy seemed to immediately doze off when handed a set of headlines, at least the ones from my typewriter. They were only fifteen to twenty lines of copy yet that was enough to put him automatically to sleep. I apparently had some ways to go before I caught on to this news writing business.

Billy was one of the best bosses I ever had. I congratulate him for being in management while lacking any traces of a real, genuine, know-nothing TOM. He eventually ended up running the whole National Radio shebang.

The wretches of UPI's Thermos World were followed by "the Dayside All-Stars," a mix of TOMs, a star writer or two, feature editors and older staffers with tons of seniority. Tim Korrigan was my favorite Dayside All-Star. Tim was short, walked like Charlie Chaplin and was incredibly predictable. A sauce pot, Tim would sometimes call in sick when he got over sauced then forget about it and show up. Whenever that happened, one of us would remind him of his call. "Oh, shit," Tim would say and quickly leave.

On the days when he hadn't made a call and then forgotten about it, Tim would waddle in, squint at the wall clock, look over at me and ask, every damn morning, "What are you doing here?" Since his question never changed, neither did my answer. "I work here, Tim."

"Oh," he would say, heading for the coat room.

Despite the agony endured by the body and mind on the overnight, it made me a smarter man. I learned that a full Thermos was a necessity for survival; you always aimed for a fly's ass; some people were able to sleep on the job and get away with it; getting drunk made you forgetful; and Scotty Reston I wasn't.

3

Never Let Facts Get in the Way of a Good Story

News would occasionally rear its ugly head in northern Indiana where I lived, and I would be asked to cover it. A call late one morning told of a disgruntled employee who had walked into the office of a U.S. Steel plant in Gary and started shooting.

By the time I got there, it was all over. The alleged shooter and his victim were long gone. Before heading to the police station, I checked in with the desk and was told the front page of the *Chicago Daily News* had a story on the shooting by the paper's ace rewrite guy, Joe Dash, and could I match it? Dash had a gripping first-hand account from the victim describing what happened when the guy with the gun rushed in. I didn't do much street work and here I was scooped, embarrassed, minutes after I put on my reporter's cap. I ran off to ask the cops what the victim had told them. "No one has talked to him," an officer said. "For one thing, he can't talk. He was shot through the throat."

"Ohhhhh," I said, slowly digesting more painful lessons: some stories are too good to be true, and some journalists can't be trusted. Mr. Joe Dash wrote so convincingly and smoothly because he wasn't slowed down by the nasty little things that put bumps in your prose—facts.

I came away more satisfied with my reporting on a case of fraud at an Indiana savings and loan association in Whiting, Irene's hometown, where we were renting an apartment. The two brothers who ran the S&L had apparently kept two sets of books. While the brothers were well-liked by depositors, investigators had a different opinion of them.

After the news broke, several customers lined up to take their money out. It was a little like "It's A Wonderful Life" with Irene's family doctor, a member of the association's board, playing Jimmy Stewart and making a little speech to the crowd about there being enough money to go around and urging people to leave it where it was. Although it was a dramatic moment, I don't recall seeing anyone give up their place in line. UPI's story, with my reporting tidbits, made the front page of a Saturday edition of *The New York Times*. The National Desk in New York sent kudos to me and the Chicago bureau.

At times knowledge about mainstream newspaper reporting in the '60s could be acquired without doing any legwork at all, by merely sitting in Andy's, a bar-restaurant across the street from UPI. Working as a Dayside All-Star one week, I was having lunch at Andy's when two other Unipressers joined me. One of them said he had spent all morning chasing details of a fire that left six or seven people dead. The teller of the tale then sighed in frustration. "All black," he said.

"Too bad," the second Unipresser said, extending his sympathies.

They moved on to something else, but the Kid asked a question as I guessed you were supposed to do in news.

"Why does it matter that they are all black?"

"Not a story," I was told with no elaboration because it was assumed none was needed. Another lesson absorbed. In the 1960s black people didn't count. If you got your white ass caught in a bad fire, you'd make the newspapers. If your ass was black and caught fire, that was real tough but not news. I wish in retrospect that I had screamed "Bullshit," but I didn't. I can't recall a single black face at UPI Chicago in those days. If there had been, maybe a few white notions of what news was would have changed earlier than they did. Maybe.

Many years later, as an editor in RFE's Central Newsroom in Munich, I was sent into the field a couple of times. One of the assignments was in Geneva, the city of Calvin, for a visit in 1969 by Pope Paul VI. The Pope's trip featured a speech at the International Labor Organization and meetings with officials of that U.N. agency. My chief responsibility was to make sure excerpts from the Pope's speech got fed promptly to the RFE audio department, freeing up the Geneva correspondent to focus on stories on what the Pope did and said and how he was welcomed.

The night before the Pope was to arrive, Jon, our man in Geneva, was sitting at a teletype keyboard, writing snippets of copy and saving the teletype tape to file to Munich later. I asked him what he was writing. "Descriptions of the Pope's welcome" was his reply. Ah, I thought, this is how the titans of the business on this side of the water do it. The Pope arrives tomorrow but why wait? Let's string some clichés together tonight about people waving and cheering as the Pope's motorcade passes. Excellent. Full disclosure: I thought it was one of the dumbest things I had ever seen.

Jon liked a calm life, at work and at home, and figured he could cut down on the pressure the next day by getting all the arrival color and hoopla out of the way the night before. What would he have filed to Munich if a crazy lady ran up to the Pope's motorcade, in those days before smothering security, and lifted her skirt? "EXTRA, EXTRA. SWISS MISS SHOWS ALL TO PETER'S SUCCESSOR."

Who knows?

When Pope Paul arrived in Geneva, they might as well have been playing "Silent night, holy night, all is calm." There wasn't a soul on the street or for that matter a sole. Genevans didn't give two shits about the Pope. The city of Calvin told him to buzz off. But wait, you ask, what happened to all those wonderful, colorful descriptions composed the night before about the enthusiastic welcome and the roaring crowds? Grow up! Jon sent them to the desk in Munich. Never let facts get in the way of a good story. (And never use the word "pontiff" if you can avoid it.)

I made sure RFE's audio crew quickly got the material it needed, holding up my end of the deal. After returning to Munich, I was asked what the Pope's reception was really like. Reuters, I was informed by one of the senior editors in Central News, had reported there was no one on the street while good old Jon had all this cheering and carrying on.

"He wrote it the night before," I said.

"Ahhh, that explains it," the senior editor said. Whether it was ever mentioned to Jon, I don't know. Nor do I remember what the folks in Munich ended up putting on the RFE wire about the Pope's welcome. I'll bet it was copy from Reuters not Jon's.

4

From A (The Magic of Radio) to Z ("Fuck Radio")

If you were lucky enough to grow up in a small town in Indiana in the '50s with a father who let you borrow the car at night, you believe in magic. It was right there at your fingertips. Flip on the radio and some smoothy hundreds of miles away would be playing Buddy Morrow's "Night Train" or a classical piece you might be able to identify years later as "Eine Kleine Nachtmusik" by Buddy Mozart.

You never wanted to get out of the car, to go home, to turn off the music. With a dollar's worth of gas, you cruised. Around and around the square. Out by the drive-in restaurant. By Linda Pickering's house, which conveniently was only a couple of doors away from Alice Pogue's, both of them lookers who you dated a few times. Over by the high school. Out by the best excuse for a supermarket in town. Back again, around the square. Around and around.

It was so dark and you were so alone. You ached but you didn't know why. You drove much faster than you should out by the drive-in and slower than a tractor with a full-load of hay around the square. God, you were lonely. Miserable, yet loving it. A guy I remember as Bill Cason from WWL, way down in New Orleans, made sure of that.

Bill was talking to you and playing Jerry Lee Lewis followed by the Modern Jazz Quartet. If Bill wasn't riding along with you, then it probably was Jay Andres at WBBM in Chicago with American Airlines's "Music 'Til Dawn." Bill talked like where he was from, the South. Jay talked like God. I loved them both.

This was long before owners of commercial radio stations couldn't make a decision so they had focus groups do it for them, long before almost every owner's goal was to make sure his station sounded exactly like every other station with the same format and long before imagination wasn't encouraged and much of the magic vanished.

This fascination with listening to something coming through the air from far away never leaves you. Someone walks into a studio, a red light goes on, words are spoken and are heard, somehow, miles and miles away—at a Texaco station on Alhambra Avenue in Frankfort, Indiana; in a '53 Dodge moseying toward an A&W in Ames, Iowa; in the kitchen of a tiny house alongside Claysville Road outside Hartsburg, Missouri.

To this day you remember how good it felt to finally have a newscast you had written read by a network anchor. The few times you had heard announcers at Chicago stations read a story of yours from UPI's radio wire they sounded uncomfortable. Was it lousy writing? Or them? Or both? Then in 1965 Ron Cochran, a veteran New York anchor, was handed the first five-minute newscast you wrote for ABC Radio News, and he made it sing. It may have been dreadful copy, but Cochran sure knew how to disguise any blemishes.

I was pretty proud of what I was doing. Kid McCoy was no longer a kid. He had made it to New York, made it to a network before he was thirty years old. If reporters who appeared frequently on ABC television were reluctant to file for radio without protest or prompting, I was unaware of it. Fifteen years later, on my second tour at CBS News, television was clearly the king and radio was dogshit, at best. Correspondents covering a good story routinely ignored radio's needs and no one—from the president of CBS News on down—did anything about it.

Many correspondents almost never filed for radio unless they had written a piece for television. Even then they usually just read their TV script, making a few minor changes and shortening it. If the Evening News passed on a piece (decided they didn't want it), radio was often out of luck. Having been turned down by Evening News, a reporter could be upset and in no mood to do anything for anyone, least of all those dirt bags in radio. Although radio had broadcasts twenty-four hours a day and was hungry for fresh pieces, many times that didn't mean squat to a reporter whose story couldn't be squeezed into the limited time on the Evening News. Radio got nothing. (A BBC radio editor once told me they had the same problem with TV reporters in his shop.)

A CBS News correspondent in one of the largest countries in the world was notorious for seldom doing anything for radio. Despite being paid mega-bucks, this correspondent often said "ehhh" if the desk called about a story seen on one of the wire services. If the correspondent was in a real talkative mood, you might get, "Ehhh. It's not ready yet. It needs to develop a little more." News, apparently, was like cheese — it needed to age a while before it was ready.

Why was this tolerated? I wasn't the only one in radio asking this. I suggested to my bosses that this person should be named secretary of state and flown to the latest international trouble spot and, presto, all would soon be quiet. Nothing would be going on. Yes, that's preposterous. So is the fact that this correspondent got away with not filing for radio, or did for many years.

I sent an email in early 1997 to Andrew Heyward, the president of CBS News, complaining about one big name correspondent who had told Radio no "so many times (that) editors and producers have either stopped asking him or do so only after much prodding from the New York desk and with great reluctance." It was inexcusable, I argued. At CBS News these days TV correspondents are more accessible to the radio crew than they usually were when I was there. I had always argued that reporters would file regularly for radio when the head of CBS News made it clear they had to. That apparently has now happened with Jeff Fager in charge. This is also an era where news organizations brag about their various platforms and how all hands contribute as often as they can to each of them. Of course, whether the quality of the product under such a heavy workload is always worth bragging about is another matter.

Admittedly, the editors and writers at CBS Radio News could be real pains in the ass. In addition to news on the hour, we did short broadcasts on breaking news called Updates. These were usually at thirty-one past the hour, but three or more Updates an hour would be done on a monster story. You go through a lot of material doing that. Radio didn't always have to have a polished piece, a reporter didn't have to struggle for hours to painfully match words to pictures. We could do quite well and were very happy chipmunks if we could simply talk to the reporter for five or ten minutes, interviewing her or him about what they knew, what they didn't know and, most important of all, what they had seen. One correspondent referred to radio as "Jaws." After doing a phone interview with the tape room, she would tell her producer, "Jaws has been fed."

What many executives in the news division thought for a long time of the radio news operation was never clearer than the afternoon of January 13, 1982 when an Air Florida plane crashed into the 14th Street Bridge in Washington DC. A reporter who had seen the wreckage was being interviewed as part of radio's special live coverage. Naturally, television wanted him too. When the reporter kept talking to radio, the vice president then in charge of the Washington bureau said, "fuck radio" and demanded that the reporter hang up the phone with us and get hooked up with the television side.

Several CBS News correspondents almost always remembered radio and didn't need coaxing. They included: Allen Pizzey, Barry Petersen, Dan Rather (when he was on scene at a major event), Susan Spencer, Marvin Kalb, David Dick and the entire Los Angeles bureau, perhaps because reporters from California were on the road a lot, and, to keep up on the news, they turned on the radio. They identified with it and apparently liked it.

The favorite alibi for not filing, frequently relayed to the radio desk around four p.m. Eastern time, was that the correspondent was "crashing" to finish a piece for the CBS Evening News, which aired two and one half hours later. That's one real long crash.

Although all our paychecks said "CBS" on them, far too many of those in television—correspondents, producers, assignment editors, coffee mugs, you name it—acted as if they considered themselves filets mignons while those of us in radio were out and out weenies.

My personal weenie status was brought home to me in late 1972 when I was among the horde of journalists at a medical facility in Kansas City waiting for Harry S Truman to die. Whenever there was an update on Truman's condition, I helped a reporter working for both television and radio pick a sound bite and file a report to the radio desk.

After working all day with the guy, I saw him one night in a bar. Here we were once again shoulder-to-shoulder. He didn't know me. He wouldn't look at me, nod or say a word. Fine. Whether the filets mignons of television knew it or not the feeling among us radio weenies was mutual: "fuck television."

5

Weighing in on Anchors

"Anchor n. A heavy object...."
— *The American Heritage Dictionary*

It was the biggest office I had ever seen. The carpet, the longest. That maroon beauty could have covered a football field. Standing at his desk where the goal posts would be was Paul Harvey, ABC Radio's superstar. He walked fifty yards to meet me, extended his hand and said, "Welcome aboard."

The Chicago Bureau manager had been kind enough to escort me from his suitcase of an office into Harvey's after telling me I had a job waiting at ABC News in New York. Thousands, including my dad, never missed Paul Harvey's midday broadcast. If you stopped at a traffic light in the Midwest on a hot summer day before cars were air conditioned, Harvey's deep, distinctive staccato was heard through the open windows all around you.

Harvey was a news entertainer — years before the Ken and Barbie infestation overran local TV stations across the country — a solo act who read for fifteen minutes a riveting mix of hard news, funny stories, commercials, clever bumper stickers, advances in medicine, farming, and technology, quotes from the Rev. Billy Graham, praise for his wife "Angel" and accounts of where he and his "traveling microphone" were or were headed next.

There were no sound bites. It was all Paul Harvey talking, and all of it done like no one else did it. Harvey truly knew how to write for the ear. Repetition was one key. He repeated things — a word, a sentence or a phrase leading up to a punch line or a silly statement by a politician or bureaucrat. And the Harvey pauses. No one I've ever heard on the radio used the pause so effectively or so often. There were long pauses between stories and in the middle of stories. After some pauses, you thought you were about to hear a new story, but no, he wasn't done with the previous one and hit you with the punch line or with an even more ludicrous comment from the moronic politician or bureaucrat of the day. The repetitions and the pauses gave listeners time to let things sink in.

A year or so after walking across his fine carpet, I was a copy editor in New York and engaged in occasional phone battles with Harvey's producer over news out of Vietnam. The calls were made when there was a story that I thought absolutely had to be on Harvey's midday newscast. At the height of the war, New York anchors crammed their war stories with specifics about casualties, armaments and geography, most of which were probably lost on listeners. After one of my calls, Harvey said something like this on the air: "Big battle near Da Nang today. Some dead, some wounded. Some of theirs, some of ours."

That was indeed the story I had asked Harvey to include. His wording may be too simplistic for some, but he told it better, tighter (always important in radio) and clearer than anything we would have churned out in New York. After that, I tried to limit my calls to Chicago. (Yes, I bitched about Harvey doing too many unimportant stories. But he had fifteen minutes to fill all by himself, and he didn't go bonkers over the couplings or uncouplings of smutty starlets and airheads. Plus he wrote so damn well that you knew something that would catch your interest was only a pause away.)

Before being promoted to editor, empowering me to make those calls to Chicago, I spent a lot of time with and learned a lot from Don Gardiner, the anchor of the network's major morning drive broadcast, "News Around The World." The fifteen-minute broadcast was put together by a producer (me, at times), a writer and an editor. Don sat by the editor's desk, stopwatch in hand, as copy was handed to him, reading and timing it.

"I need ten seconds in the top," he would say. This was new ground for me. At UPI we put items on the radio wire every hour never worrying about how they could be squeezed into a newscast. That was up to those at the other end to figure out. Thankfully, the writer of "News Around The World" knew how to come up in a hurry with the additional ten seconds of script Don needed. I never had much of a clue, either as a rookie or an old guy, how to "write for time" as it's called.

Don once pulled me aside with that day's script and pointed to the tape intros I had written as the producer. Of the ten pieces of tape, eight of the lead-ins were identical. "President Johnson had this to say," "Senator Aiken had this to say," "General Westmoreland had this to say," etc. Was I a whiz at this writing biz or what?

When Don talked you listened, on air and off. He was a fine writer and wrote his five-minute newscasts but not his first broadcast of the day, "News Around The World." That allowed him to get an extra hour or two of sleep and allowed ABC to use him on the air later in the day.

ABC Radio had a roster of young, talented anchor-reporters, including Don Allen, Steve Bell, Mort Crim, Jim Harriott, Ted Koppel (more about Ted in the next chapter) and Charles Osgood. I can still hear a haunting piece Bell did walking on a balcony at the Lorraine Motel in Memphis shortly after Martin Luther King, Jr. was assassinated.

Peter Jennings, the new and unready anchor of ABC-TV's evening news, came to radio a few minutes before noon to read a newscast. This was in his pretty boy phase, before he made the commitment to become a serious journalist. I remember Jennings behind the mike in the radio studio, flipping through the pages of a New York tabloid as the tapes on his newscast played. He wasn't really there, a remarkable contrast to the fine, intelligent anchorman he later became.

At CBS News, Dallas Townsend was the epitome of a dedicated, no nonsense anchor. For years Dallas wrote every line of copy for "The CBS World News Roundup," the network's well-regarded fifteen-minute morning newscast. Dallas had a time-saving shortcut: abbreviations. An editor handed a Townsend script might see:

> "T Pres speaks in Wash tdy to t AMA convention, a group tt has soundly criticized his health spending plans. We hear about tt from WH Corr Rbt Pierpoint."

Most mornings at ten Eastern time Townsend did two broadcasts—a live five-minute newscast to most of the country, and an updated version of the "World News Roundup" to the West Coast on tape. Because of a breaking story one morning, it was decided that Townsend would have to do most of the West Coast Roundup live. About three minutes to ten, a summer relief anchor, Dave Dugan, was handed Dallas's script for the hourly news, abbreviations galore. It was too late to tense up. Dugan read it flawlessly and was applauded when he walked back into the newsroom. I trust that somewhere in the script there was the word "commence," one of Dallas's favorites. In his world, talks or visits didn't "start," they "commence." He may have been the last American anchor to say that in a newscast. I know he is the last person I ever saw smoking unfiltered Lucky Strikes.

Little Pictures

The elegance and class I had always associated with CBS News from the outside was personified once I was inside by a veteran anchor, Allan Jackson. Tall, lean and with the bearing of an ambassador, Jackson was perhaps best known for his Saturday morning newscasts sponsored by Chevrolet. Many my age can still sing the "See the USA in your Chevrolet" jingle from those days. After a broadcast, you would occasionally see Jackson zipping up his pants. He had loosened his belt for breathing purposes before going on the air.

Jackson had help from a writer in doing the "Morning Report," a daily broadcast focusing on a top story. I was called in on overtime the day after George Wallace, the Alabama governor and would-be president, was shot. The "Morning Report" writer picked a newsy topic — pretty simple the day I was on — read whatever he could find on it and then produced a script that Jackson re-wrote. I pounded out a several-page opus, indignant in tone, that recapped what was known about the Wallace shooting, tossed in all the usual platitudes about guns being as available in America as M&Ms and blamed everyone and his brother for the shooting.

Jackson threw most of my bilious diatribe into the garbage — thank you very much — and turned out a small gem that concluded, "As long as public figures appear in public places, the loner will have a chance to strike. But it is the loner that is sick — not society." Being a diplomat, he later thanked me before suggesting that radio was a place where it was best to try to "paint little pictures." Sweeping, grandiose endeavors came out muddled. Little pictures stayed with you.

I never forgot that and preached it constantly as a TOM at CBS. A freelance reporter sent to cover a hurricane in the South kept phoning in pieces about "debris all over" and "houses crumbled like matchsticks," the usual clichés when talking about any bad storm. No little pictures that set this one apart.

I got on the phone to the reporter, strung together many graphic terms ("asshole" probably being among them) and made it clear we were hoping for something better. Before he had a chance to return the compliment, I asked, "For God's sakes, isn't there something you're seeing that makes this different?"

"You know," he said, "there is one odd thing. Everywhere you go it smells like pine. And I asked around and people down here say that's because of all the pine trees snapped in half." Bingo. Little pictures.

Jackson and Townsend were among the thoroughbreds who made CBS News, Radio the best there was for many years. During my time there I worked with several other well-known and respected newscasters, including Douglas Edwards, Reid Collins, John Hart and Christopher Glenn as well as Jackie Judd, Judy Muller and Deborah Potter whose talents we'll talk about later.

Edwards, the first anchor of an evening news broadcast on CBS-TV, was as dapper in person as he appeared and sounded on the air. You almost never saw him without his suit coat on. It had to be an extremely hot day for Doug to take the coat off. If he did, you'd notice right away something was different when you came into the newsroom. Doug was an old school gentleman and broadcaster. He cupped his right ear while reading radio newscasts and didn't think listeners should have to cover their ears because of something he said. I went into the studio one afternoon with a story about J.D. Salinger getting a divorce. He wouldn't use it, telling me later, "I don't like to do stories about people's private lives." He wouldn't have much trouble fitting in today, would he?

One of the younger CBS anchors was Reid Collins who replaced Townsend on the Roundup after affiliates agitated for Dallas's removal because he "sounded old," a perception that is the kiss of death in commercial broadcasting. Reid *was* a livelier broadcaster than Dallas; his delivery brisker and his writing more colorful and contemporary. He was fond of toying with words and cleverly weaving popular song titles into his copy. He once slipped "livin' on Tulsa time" into a story, and it made the item better and more interesting.

Collins was also better than Townsend at computer disposal. This takes some s'plainin'. Despite CBS's reputation as the Tiffany network, the radio operation was "Nanook Of The North" when it came to equipment. Long after most radio outlets at every level were using tape cartridges to put sound on the air, CBS stuck with what it had always been comfortable with—bulky Ampex machines with their large reels of tape. After a tour of CBS Radio's facilities on West 57th Street, several Japanese broadcasters were reported to have said they enjoyed "seeing the radio museum."

CBS News was also slow in moving into the computer age. After the News Division finally bought computers, they were introduced gradually with some people using them immediately while others still banged away on typewriters. Collins made it clear he wasn't in love with the change and was among the last of the typewriter contingent. After training sessions and a shakedown period, a date was set for a switch over to an all-computer newsroom. When Collins arrived that morning and saw a computer terminal instead of a typewriter on his desk, he picked up the computer, placed it in the wastebasket and left.

Reid was suspended. Not long afterward, he went to CNN in Washington as a morning anchor, reading copy he wrote on a typewriter. Eventually he was told to "get with the program" and started using a computer. As CNN and Collins were negotiating, one executive reportedly said, "and make sure you hire his writer." The TOM from CNN didn't seem to know much about radio "talent." Most radio anchors usually wrote what they read on the air. Television anchors, doing longer broadcasts, needed writers. Being smooth in front of a camera didn't mean you were handy with a keyboard. Many TV anchors were, to be kind, mediocre wordsmiths.

Fortunately, there were exceptions. John Hart was one. The anchor of the CBS-TV morning news could certainly write and expected good copy from his writers. For several months, I had the privilege of writing a nine a.m. Eastern time radio cast for Hart, which he read after his TV show. There's a lot of blowing off about broadcasters who deliver the news in a conversational style. Hart actually did it. I remember writing a story for him along these lines one morning:

"Some men in Northern Ireland put razors in their pockets and hoods over their heads and went out last night and beat up a 17-year-old Catholic girl who had been dating a Protestant boy. They carved a cross on her forehead."

It was a challenge to write for him, forcing yourself to loosen up and to tell stories in a more casual way than you did for most anchors — casual in style, not casual with the facts. The radio writer who wrote the nine a.m. for Hart began the day turning out a newscast for Dallas Townsend and ended it helping Richard C. Hottelet with one — three very different anchors with their own approaches to telling the news.

Although I liked the shift and found it rewarding, I didn't like the hours — a four a.m. start — and decided to return to Radio Free Europe in Munich where I had worked for a couple of years before getting homesick and being hired by CBS. Hart left CBS in the mid '70s for NBC and dropped out of commercial broadcasting in 1988. "It doesn't do to jazz up the news," he said on his departure from NBC to do a program on the Discovery Channel for *The Christian Science Monitor*. "It doesn't do to exploit the bizarre so regularly that it seems to be the norm," *The Pittsburgh Press* quoted him as saying. "It doesn't do to condense an event so much that there's no room for information, only characterization." This was back in 1988, way before any of us had heard of reality TV, Lindsay Lohan, Snooki or the Kardashian septuplets.

Another wonderful broadcast writer was Christopher Glenn. Many people in and out of the business talked about Glenn's great "pipes" — "a bedroom voice," in the words of one manager — but the raves should have been just as loud for the way he put sentences together. Unlike many anchors, he wasn't afraid to use his ample vocabulary. When I questioned the choice of a long word in his copy one time, he responded, "Let's use the language."

He was right. Chris didn't simply read words. He picked words that reverberated with that marvelous voice. They were well-chosen words, they fit. If Chris said "there was a scuffle," the way he said it made you hear furniture being kicked across the floor. That's very special.

Chris was known to an entire generation for his television work on "In The News," a program for kids, and that may explain why his name popped up occasionally in crossword puzzles. Sure, he didn't make it as many times as Mel Ott, Arthur Ashe or the Alou brothers, yet it's a kick to discover someone you see every day as the answer in a crossword puzzle.

Glenn, who died only months after retiring in 2006, anchored many space shots, most notably the Challenger explosion. His shocked "oh, a great tragedy here" near the top of the broadcast captured the stunned emotions of that day.

Chris took over from Douglas Edwards as anchor of "The World Tonight," for years a major evening radio broadcast, and closed his career anchoring "The CBS World News Roundup" in the mornings.

I occasionally wrote or edited copy for Ed Bradley, Morton Dean, and John Roberts who anchored television newscasts on weekends. Bradley, Dean and Roberts came over to radio to read a newscast written for them and always asked questions if something in the script wasn't clear to them or well explained, a habit not universal among TV types.

Among the other big names I dealt with from time to time: Bob Schieffer, an artist at heart, who drew intriguing faces in the margins of his radio scripts; Steve Kroft who in his pre-"60 Minutes" days complained politely about how many changes I made in his copy ; and Lesley Stahl who once declined to walk across the street to the radio studios for an interview about a piece she had on that week's "60 Minutes," insisting that we talk to her on the telephone. That would have made sense if she were stuck in western Bangladesh rather than on West 57th Street.

When I became a TOM at CBS, I thought it was time to deal with a veteran broadcaster who for years had been doing sloppy newscasts. Among his sins, as I saw them: not spending enough time on his broadcast; writing too many long and very predictable international items; trying sometimes to ad-lib a story from notes he had taken on a reporting assignment earlier in the day; and occasionally not being in the studio when his show began. Outside of that, his newscasts were fine.

I went into attack mode, talked to him and sent him memos, eventually one memo too many, one that said the anchor was "cheating" the audience. A vice president of CBS News, not my immediate boss but obviously my superior, came charging into my office and informed me I could not write a note like that to a CBS News correspondent and had to apologize. I doubt that this vice president heard many radio newscasts. If he had, he might have realized the problems with the correspondent. Following orders, I wrote an apology, a wishy-washy one, but before the day was over my boss, another vice president, stopped by to show his support. I'm sure he thought I was on the right track. My memory would like me to believe the anchor's newscasts became less disjointed after this run-in, but I'm not sure that's true.

One of the most efficient anchors I knew was Dick Reeves. A

marvelous writer, Dick started working on a script immediately when asked to do something on short notice. Some anchors claimed they couldn't write anything until they knew what tape they were going to get. Not Dick. He knew he had to tell the story with or without tape, so he got to it and kept adjusting his script to fit the latest tape to reach his desk. Anchors who waited until the tape arrived ran the risk of disaster or a near miss when the on-air light went on. Despite being urged to watch how Reeves did it, some anchors stuck to their own, last-second way of doing things, resulting in some rocky broadcasts, both in terms of production and editorial content.

David Dow, George Herman, David Jackson, Bill Lynch, Frank Settipani and Nick Young were among the other CBS News anchors who wrote good copy for the ear and could handle any story, big or small.

A Salute to Bill Whitney

In all my years in the business, the most amazing anchor day in and day out was Bill Whitney. He was the same every day and every hour of every day. Regardless of what was going on around him at CBS, Bill was Mr. Calm. Editors screaming at people in the tape rooms or at desk assistants, an anchor having a pissing match with a desk assistant or editor, ten television sets blaring, tapes for upcoming broadcasts being played at full volume on speakers all over the newsroom, someone yelling that the food order from the deli was at the front desk—none of that distracted Bill. He was quietly doing his job as though he were sitting on a deck at home, writing a letter to an old friend.

Bill wrote clearly, read well, knew what was news, knew what to leave out (very important), was always careful about sourcing and understood how to effectively incorporate sounds from an event so the ear and mind got a better grasp of the story. In the newscasts of too many anchors, these same sounds become unexplained noise.

He handled without complaint or flinching late stories or a sound bite on a breaking story that didn't get processed until minutes to air time, and, perhaps most impressive of all, he didn't get flustered or try to blame anyone when a piece of sound he had been promised several times mysteriously never made its way to him before the broadcast. In similar circumstances, there were anchors, male and female, who lost it big time and never got over it for the rest of their shift.

I may be partial to Bill because the two of us helped change the way CBS News, Radio handled major news stories that weren't quite big enough to interrupt affiliate programming with a BULLETIN. Bill, the radio newsroom and I put together the first CBS News Update, although all these years later none of us can remember what the story was. Previously at CBS a good breaking story would be covered on hourly newscasts and in one or two Special Reports during the day. These specials were four or five minutes long, had a title—say "Showdown at the SALT Talks"—and were put together by a producer-writer given two to four hours to do it. Both the process and the product often struck me as slow and pompous.

An Update was usually produced in twenty-five minutes or less, ran about a minute-and-a-half to two minutes and didn't have a title. The anchor just said "CBS News Update" and got rolling. Joe Dembo, the vice president for radio news, gave the go ahead for the Update format, which proved popular with CBS affiliates and with the staff. CBS is now committed to doing an Update at thirty-one past every hour, taking some of the spontaneity and seat-of-the pants excitement out of the process I suspect.

A closing word about Whitney who is still heard on CBS News, Radio. He is human and has a weakness. Sports. Absolutely clueless. He knows as much about popular American sports as I do about the history of crocheting in the Azores.

If I ever went back into broadcasting—and I won't—I'd want it to be with Bill. This time around we'd rig up for him one of those wristbands like the NFL quarterbacks have listing all the plays and print on Bill's the pronunciations of some of the trickier names in sports. We'd do some solid newscasts and, best of all, have some fun too.

6

"They Didn't Have That Shirt in Your Size?"

Ted Koppel is the first person I ever heard use that put down. Koppel skewered me with it in the early '60s for my jelly belly, and it's still one of my favorites. Even back then in the ABC Radio newsroom in New York, Ted was a dozen notches above the rest of us. He was smarter, funnier, wrote better, handled pressure better and, yes, had thicker hair.

Damn if Ted wasn't younger too. And best of all, he was easy to work with if you were competent, and, despite a few major lapses, I've always thought I was. Granted he wasn't a star then, but I hear from ex-ABC news people who were around him much longer than I was that Ted never changed in that regard.

Which brings us to Dan Rather. Sorry. The man invites cheap shots like ants on a half-eaten Snickers bar, as a certain Texan might say. When someone crossed him, Rather was fond of saying, "I don't want their job." Translation: suspend the bastard. The producer of "Dan Rather Reporting," a daily news and analysis radio program on CBS, found that out after she challenged Dan's version of the lyrics to "The Gambler," the song made famous by Kenny Rogers.

In an ad-lib to his script, Rather messed up part of the lines about you've got to "know when to hold'em, know when to fold'em." Confident she was right, the producer pointed out the mistake to Rather. He said he knew his country music. Dan always got his way and his way, the wrong way, was what ended up on the air. The producer, who in fact knew her country music better than Rather, was punished for daring to challenge him, told that the mighty anchorman didn't want to see her face for the rest of the week.

That's justice in the world of an eight hundred-pound gorilla. Rather didn't tell her to get lost. An underling did, my boss, Larry Cooper. It wasn't the finest hour of the two Larrys in radio management. Old number two, me, didn't get any calls from the big suits at CBS. When told about the "problem," I believe they went straight to the number one Larry and put the squeeze on him.

I am now required by the U.S. penal code as well as the standard journalism practice known as "Staying with the Herd" to relate at least one example from personal experience of how strange Rather could be. Ready?

Some evenings he would stop by the radio desk and chat with an anchor or whoever else was around. I was whoever else one night and found myself having a conversation—actually he was talking and I was listening—about a personal income tax bill being considered by Congress. In discussing the possible impact of the bill, Rather, the millionaire, mentioned how some people try to escape paying taxes and then said, "if that were you or I" we would certainly be caught should we try to cheat. He gave the impression that the anchor and managing editor of the CBS Evening News was in the same tax bracket as the executive editor of radio. Close, Dan, but not quite.

Before becoming a TOM, I wrote and produced "Dan Rather Reporting" several times and luckily had no run-ins with him over country music or anything else. While Walter Cronkite was the CBS Evening News anchor, I also filled in as writer-producer of his radio commentary. Once, after reading the first couple of paragraphs of my script about turmoil in the Philippines, Cronkite said, "That's a good start." While the rest may have truly sucked, I sure remember those four words. I can't recall another word he ever said to me.

Charles Osgood is another big name I occasionally wrote or edited copy for. My resumé resembles Charlie's ever so slightly in that we both worked first at ABC Radio and then went to CBS. Although he's a terrific person and a clever, inventive writer, I don't think Charlie should ever have agreed—nor should he ever have been asked—to read commercials on the radio. He doesn't do commercials on television as the anchor of "CBS News Sunday Morning," so why does he do them on radio? Because the ladies and lords of the radio division wanted him to so CBS Radio would, once again, fall into lockstep with what ABC was doing. Paul Harvey, the colossus at ABC Radio, did his own commercials in his broadcasts and therefore Osgood should too. There were big bucks to be made.

Journalists—even poetry-writing, banjo-playing ones—are paid to remain outwardly impartial. Don Imus and Kiefer Sutherland do commercials. Journalists don't. They don't sell things or endorse grape juice and treadmills as Charlie has.

Last and least, let's talk about Bill O'Reilly. According to a Fox News website, O'Reilly "takes naps" in his spare time. I thought he was doing exactly that at CBS-TV News during the brief time the two of us rubbed shoulders.

As assistant northeast bureau manager, I asked him one evening to cover brush fires in New Jersey, which I thought might make a piece for the Morning News. It was admittedly not the greatest of stories, but you don't get to pick your parents and reporters in their first network job don't get to select their stories. When I told O'Reilly where I thought he should go (that just came out of my keyboard, and I'm leaving it), he suggested the crew should go alone and he would "look" at the tape when they got back. Granted I was new to television, but the journalist in me thought an eager reporter ought to get a first-hand look at what he was reporting on, that any tape brought back by the crew wouldn't tell him all the story, that if he went to the scene he might get a feel for what was going on—a sense of its impact or lack of—and might find a nugget, a compelling element that could be the focus of a story prompted by what a witness or fire official told him up close and personal.

My recollection is that he ended up going with the crew, still I was put off by what I saw as his lack of interest in the details of a story that might get him on the Morning News. I believe his piece did make the broadcast but don't most reporters want to do what they are paid to do, report stories?

O'Reilly's troubles at CBS News during the Falklands War—he was angry that footage of a riot he and his crew had covered was folded, uncredited, into a piece by Bob Schieffer—didn't stop him from moving on to other networks and eventually becoming the mega hit he is today, both as a TV personality and the author of several best-selling books. In discussing his books, he was quoted by *The New York Times* as saying "nobody edits me," an attitude that sits real well with this old copy editor. I guess I've got it all wrong. Everyone but Bill O'Reilly needs an editor.

Yo, Mr. O'Bill, you never write something that couldn't be improved, said a little more precisely or explained a little better? YOU don't want to be edited? Hardly anyone does. It can hurt, but it can also really help.

My younger brother, his reasoning powers perhaps diminished by lolling in the California sun too long, thinks "The O'Reilly Factor" is television at its best. My TV viewing is mainly sports, sports, sports and old movies. Real, stimulating macho confrontation takes place in a sports arena, I think. Two people interrupting and insulting each other neither fascinates nor enlightens me. The little I have seen of "The O'Reilly Factor" and that infuriating quote from *The New York Times* lead me to paraphrase Ted Koppel and ask O'Reilly, "They didn't have a hat in your size?"

7

Many a Master Doesn't Have a Master's

*J*ulius Caesar knew what he was talking about when he said, "All newsrooms are divided into three parts."

There are a few very good pros who can handle anything and everything and are itching to. In the middle is a good-sized group, ranging from the pretty good to the so-so, who keep the place above water on slow days and hectic ones. The last rung is a tiny hopeless/ helpless bunch, typically top-heavy with seniority and lacking any trace of creativity or the most basic prerequisite of a good journalist: curiosity. If they had a motto, it would be "we don't know, and we don't care that we don't know." These people come in hoping nothing will happen before they go home and praying that they won't be asked to do a complex story, either write it or interview someone about it. Why they decided to get into journalism is mystifying. To both them and almost everyone else. Perhaps there were already enough funeral home directors.

In this age when universities have lumped Journalism and Media Studies into the same department as Public Relations, many journalism courses are taught by people with doctorates. I'm delighted to say that the best newsman I ever met never went beyond the eighth grade. Jim Edwards worked for Radio Free Europe and wrote some of the simplest, clearest copy I've ever seen. He was the Paris bureau manager for RFE for many years until, against his wishes, he was moved to the Munich headquarters where he became director of news.

I was running RFE's English-language news desk the night French President Georges Pompidou died. I called Jim, thinking he would like to know. A few minutes later he was sitting at a desk behind me, writing pieces on Pompidou — who he was, what he stood for.

Jim's brilliance as a writer was his ability to choose exactly the right words, the fewer the better. This carried over into his days as news director. A top TOM in the Central Newsroom was sent to a major international conference on human rights and kept filing stories that I thought badly missed the point, so I rewrote most of them. He called one day to talk to Jim and asked, "What do the desks think of my copy?" Jim's reply? "They like what they have been getting."

In those pre-laptop computer days, it wasn't until the manager-reporter returned to Munich that he saw how I had "butchered" his pieces. He wasn't happy, but Jim's careful choice of words showed his confidence in me. Jim always gave me lots of rope and for that I'm grateful.

Jim was one of several talented people who, ignoring my steady stream of smart-ass comments, helped me become a better journalist. Bob Buckhorn, an editor at UPI's National Radio wire, was the first person to talk to me about my news writing, the first to explain the editing he had done. Bob would scoot his chair over to me with my copy in hand and tell me what he had taken out and why, what he had put in and why. I remember him saying that good radio copy had a pace to it. Most of my stuff didn't. I wasn't sure what he meant at the time, but I watched closely how he reshaped my writing, and I made a point of looking at pieces he had written for the wire.

When I landed at ABC Radio News, Ken Scott was the editorial maestro in the main tape room in early mornings. I had never been in a network tape room before. It was incredibly busy and noisy yet Ken was clearly in full control. He was fast in deciding what cuts he wanted the technician to make, and he could do three or five things at once: taking in pieces from a correspondent and timing them; typing up information about the report or sound bite, including the incue and the outcue; relaying information from the desk to the reporter in the field; and making sure the cuts got out to the desk for immediate consideration. He was truly a master.

On the ABC copy desk much of the time was Nick George, the best broadcast editor I ever saw. He could tear apart a newscast thirty seconds to air and get all the elements to mesh without a catastrophe.

Shortly after I started at ABC, I was hanging around the copy desk when Nick asked, "What are you?" I told him what shift I was on. "You're nothing," Nick said, "you're at lunch." He favored corncob pipes and preached using simple language. "Don't search for synonyms" was one of his maxims. Anyone who worked with him had that one and others pounded into them.

Tony Brunton hired me twice at CBS, the first time as a writer and then, after my second stint with RFE, as an editor. He called me about once a year in Munich to ask if I was still happy there. Tony was an accomplished and thorough planner, setting up radio coverage for political conventions, presidential visits overseas, spectacular criminal trials and major breaking stories. After I joined him as a manager at CBS Radio, he may have regretted making those calls. I never listened to Tony as much as I should have about the need to plan things. I was from the let's-jump-into-the-water-and-see-what-happens school. He was smarter than that and wanted no part of it.

Squeezed in between my time as an editor and then a manager at CBS Radio, came my brief spell in television as assistant northeast bureau manager. In that job I was sent to El Salvador on short notice. (Short notice being I was asked one afternoon if I had a passport and the next afternoon I was in San Salvador.) I had never produced a piece for TV, didn't have the slightest idea of how to go about it, yet during my two-week stay there two pieces I theoretically put together aired on CBS News. My bacon was saved by Terry Forgette, a freelance tape editor, who knew his business and let me ride on his coattails. I had expected to stay in El Salvador a lot longer, getting much needed experience in television production, until my mother called one morning to tell me my dad had a stroke. By the time I arrived back in the States several hours later, he was dead.

Not long after El Salvador, Joe Dembo, my old boss in radio, asked if I wanted to take his job as executive editor while he moved up to vice president of radio news. I took a long time deciding. Me and my big mouth had always thought we knew how to run a newsroom, so on a Monday morning, after a long weekend of struggling with a decision,

I told Joe "yes." I've often wondered why Joe offered me the job, what he saw in me. We never did discuss that.

Joe was a marvelous human being and wonderful to work for. He left you alone most of the time, assuming you knew what you were doing unless you proved otherwise. He thought newscasts were for news and not publicity about misbehaving starlets, which probably explains why he left commercial broadcasting in 1988. He was infuriated when air time was wasted on stunts such as the one staged every February in Punxsutawney, Pennsylvania. CBS News, Radio had a proud tradition and a passion for standards. Some in the radio business perceived those qualities as proof that we were resistant to change. Not so. Joe welcomed new ideas, and the CBS News Updates on breaking stories started under his watch are proof of that.

First-rate journalists aren't a dime a dozen and when you're lucky enough to be around one, the best thing to do is ask if there is anything you can do to help and then watch closely. Not that you want to ape their every move some day, but by careful observation you can learn how an extremely capable journalist handles things and borrow a trick or two.

Steve Baltin, a producer at CBS Radio News, comes to mind. When a big story broke, or even just a damn interesting one on a slow day, Steve lit a fire in the newsroom. He got the entire shop working the story. Editors, writers, desk assistants, anchors—all making phone calls or chasing information or suggesting angles and people to pursue. An entire newsroom trying to find out as much as it could as fast as it could. Steve's skill, enthusiasm and calmness kept a chaotic situation from becoming a mess. The jokers in local television who trumpet "team coverage" should have eye witnessed this. (Isn't all good coverage by any newsroom, team coverage, the combined efforts and talents of reporters, writers, editors, technicians and experts? Sure it is. When team coverage is ballyhooed, what is really meant is sequential reporting, reporters doing back-to-back reports on different parts of a story. I'll grant you that sequential reporting isn't exactly dripping with pizzazz, still it's a little more accurate.)

When I was at UPI, there was an explosion at an ice show in Indianapolis that killed dozens of people. An AP reporter was at the show, and AP was first with the story and got most of the play in the major newspapers the next morning. In the following news cycle, UPI pushed AP out of the way, thanks to better reporting and better writing by a talented senior deskman, David Smothers.

At RFE, Barry Griffiths, an editor-manager, was adept at taking fragments of information and speculation about a major news development, weaving in bits of background and history, and producing, in an hour or so, an understandable, clear and very readable article for the English-language wire. These are master journalists, and they're rare.

Much more common are the average Janes and Joes who work hard most of the time, usually do good work and, like any decent journalist, complain sometimes. At RFE, a competent newsman—a David Ben Gurion look-alike whose sparse hair on his head was bunched together in a bird's nest—would arrive at work, collapse into a chair and then loudly exhale "AHHHHHHH." It was painful to hear. A stranger might have immediately pushed him to the floor and started CPR. No need to. He was fine. Just a little frustrated about where he was in life (geographically, professionally and matrimonially), and once he let go a couple of long "AHHHHHHH"s, he would get down to work and do his job.

"What Does That Mean, Darrell?"

With the wire services spewing out copy virtually non-stop, it was hard to keep up in any shop, and the result at times was terrible or unintelligible stories being broadcast or published. In the cluttered room at my home where I'm writing this, there is a sign on the wall with four quotes. One about skiing ("It's all in the boots"), one about life ("Anybody that don't make mistakes doesn't do anything"), and the other two about bad journalism.

While preparing to take the desk one afternoon at RFE, I came across a story that made no sense at all, at least to me. I asked the person who had put it on the wire, "What does that mean, Darrell?" His response: "You know, I wondered about that myself." Good. He at least glanced at the thing and realized he didn't understand it. Then why in the name of sweet Jesus, did he put it on the wire? I sure don't know. It still baffles me. That exchange with Darrell is one of the quotes on the wall.

The final quote consists of ten words, seven of which came out of my typewriter. During my final months at ABC Radio, four new FM news networks were created, a decision the TOMs may have contemplated for quite a long time but which saw them delay hiring any new anchors until nearly the last second. Suddenly several strange people were in our midst. One of them had a booming voice and that was about all. While he sounded good, he wasn't much of a writer. Scratch that. He couldn't write worth shit and to compound the problem he never seemed to write enough shit.

Shortly after he began one newscast, an involved but important Supreme Court decision appeared on the wires. I decided to write a back-in lead, telling the background of the case before explaining to listeners what the court had ruled. I took the story into the studio where this deep-throated marvel added a little something of his own, the words "this just in." The fourth quote on the wall, taken from one hell of an ABC Radio broadcast, is: "This just in…four years ago the U.S. Supreme Court…."

There are bad car mechanics, bad school teachers, and probably bad brain surgeons so why shouldn't there be bad journalists? If some people weren't bad at what they do, those who are really good at it wouldn't stand out so much.

I had the honor of meeting one person who knew everything, had an opinion on everything and made damn sure, especially if you were a TOM, that you were constantly reminded of how much this person knew, which was everything. This individual would interview, say an official at the National Hurricane Center about the expected track of a storm, and then argue that it be thrown away because "the guy doesn't know what he's talking about." There would follow some indecipherable malarkey about how our big shot writer knew where the latest hurricane was headed, but the National Hurricane Center didn't and it, the Center, ought to be closed. Good. Let's close it. Now shut the fuck up and process the tape.

One of the worst "newsmen" I ever met—he apparently thought all of Southeast Asia was one country with Bangkok as its capital—later wandered into teaching journalism, "newsroom skills" he called it. Not to worry. It was in Australia, another example of a dependable ally taking one for the team. As I recall, he had a brassy voice and maybe that helped conceal the nonsense he must have spouted in front of a class. Now that I think about it that voice may have made the stupidities seem profundities. Oh shit! WARNING TO EMPLOYERS: For the next fifteen years, don't hire anyone who has taken a journalism course Down Under. It just ain't worth the risk.

8

"Hold on, Mother Teresa, While We Get You into a Studio."

The brightest people in network newsrooms were usually the desk assistants, the fresh meat hired right out of college and paid almost nothing, yet expected to know how to fix anything instantly (computers, printers, Xerox machines, chairs, coffee makers, telephones, toilets) and to be able to get any one immediately on the phone, with the possible exception of the Pope and Elvis and even then they better have a pretty damn good explanation of why neither one was taking calls.

A newsroom staffed with energetic, eager, smart DAs was a good newsroom. The best DAs soon figured out which editors, anchors, writers and managers were worth watching—those who knew what they were doing: how to chase a story; how to be careful not to say or imply on the air or in print more than was really known when a story first broke; and who never gave up trying to get basic facts on their own, refusing to wait on the wire services to do it for them. Good DAs also instinctively spotted the newsroom debris—those of every rank who had been there too long, the people you needed to work around to get anything done right.

Good editors and anchors mined these kids for their expertise about popular culture: music, movies, people, and gadgets, both technological and sexual. (Just funning in the last category there.) Kurt Cobain killed himself. Who in the world is Kurt Cobain? What the hell was it he sang? Whatever it is, Buster, get your ass in a cab over to Tower Records and hurry back with a couple of albums.

(This brings up the issue of why were middle-aged fogies scrambling to report on someone they had barely heard of, having to fake that they knew why this person mattered. The flip answer, and the only one I have, is that once Howard Stern and other shock jocks got so big—and stayed big, the ultimate male fantasy but I digress — the thinking was that all-news stations should try to grab part of that same audience by paying more attention to stars and celebrities. Things degenerated from there to a focus all too often on smut and stupid people. You might call the result Infobation, information to masturbate by.)

DAs saved many a radio newscast. The wrong tape cartridge was taken into a studio and was about to be played when a kid in chinos with a truly terrible excuse for a beard raced in with the right one. Or thirty seconds to air an anchor started to print the script for the entire newscast when the computer crashed, and this gorgeous young lady in tight clothes and long, glittering earrings somehow coaxed it back to life in ten seconds. Or a correspondent in some hell hole, unheard from for thirty-six hours, suddenly was on the phone because a team of DAs kept calling and calling until they got through and got her on the air with the latest on a big story.

Howard Stringer, who stepped down in 2013 as chief executive of the Sony Corp., is a former president of CBS, a former president of CBS News, a former executive producer of the CBS Evening News with Dan Rather, a former executive producer of CBS Reports, and a former desk assistant. During his brief tenure at WCBS-TV, Stringer was, by his own admission, the worse DA ever. His later success surely reinforces the point I always made to writers and editors about DAs: "Be good to them because you may end up working for them someday." That wasn't just a bunch of applesauce. I know at least two journalists who in mid-career found themselves taking orders from one of their ex-DAs.

It was a delight to watch a good DA in action, especially with two or more phones in hand. One of the smoothest I ever saw was a young guy with his shirt always hanging out who, when trying to track down a key person to be interviewed, would have a phone cradled on each shoulder and a third one in his hand as he kept dialing and dialing, talking to whoever answered on the other end, usually getting closer and closer to his target, snatching sips of coffee and bites of a Danish in between calls but still aware of everything else going on around him, including at times a newscast that was about to self-destruct if he didn't put one of the phones down briefly and help out.

It was this sleight of hand master, Marc Singer, who one morning shouted into a bad phone line to some desperate part of the world, "Hold on, Mother Teresa, while we get you into a studio." I don't remember why we wanted to talk to her. I do know, God bless her, that she talked to us in English. Marc, or perhaps another DA helping him, may have had to clear several linguistic hurdles before finally reaching Mother Teresa. In my experience, DAs were frequently the only ones in a network newsroom with any foreign language talents.

Like any job, it took a while to learn the lingo. Ask the new DA on duty the morning that Bill Lynch, the anchor of "The CBS World News Roundup," pushed the panic button in the studio, triggering a loud alarm near the copy editor's desk. The new kid was sent running in to see what Bill wanted. "I need a little fill," he said.

The unlucky cuss raced back to the newsroom, grabbed Charlie Osgood's producer, and shouted, "Lynch needs you in the studio right away." Bill hadn't written enough copy and needed "a little fill" — wire service stories — brought to him so he had something to read in place of dead air. Not knowing the jargon, the new DA had gone to Osgood's producer, a short guy named Phil.

Most DAs wanted to be producers, writers or anchors and were willing to pay their dues by working lousy hours for lousy wages under considerable pressure as long as this dues-paying didn't take more than a couple of years. Many blossomed and were excited about what they were doing. Always knowing the latest news, watching live feeds of major events as they happened, trying to find a scientist who had just won a Nobel Prize or a senator who had made a provocative proposal, taking calls from big name correspondents and smiling when they saw Dan Rather, Charles Kuralt or Lesley Stahl in the hall.

Some apparently thought even entry-level jobs in journalism would be like life on television — glamorous as all hell with upscale people, nifty hair styles and a fabulous wardrobe. They didn't realize that glamour is a pretty rare commodity at three a.m. and doesn't exist at all at that hour on weekends. It's the god awful middle of the night, and you're being paid to schlep tape into a studio to a technician who hasn't shaved in a week, who exists on Cokes, powdered donuts, and stale, smelly popcorn and who periodically pulls a crumb of something out of the folds of a filthy sweater and eats it. That's the attractive part. The unpleasant part is that the tech, who's wearing soiled jeans, dirty white socks and the aforementioned filthy sweater, is asleep. It's four minutes to the hour and that means you're expected to touch him so the newscast can go on. You went to an excellent college, made the Dean's List and all that, and now here you are within inches of this person who is the very reason the Salvation Army rings all those bells at Christmas time. This splash of reality really gets to some.

The DAs who ended up staying in news weren't bothered by the crumbs and dirty jeans because they found their bearer and wearer out-and-out engrossing or talented, sometimes both, and usually they were right. Those who disliked trying to rouse the dead, even with a stick, soon quit or called in sick a lot and then stopped showing up. Many of those who dropped out were fine, intelligent young people. They just weren't cut out for the grunt work and grunge that went with broadcasting. They ended up in PR or other professions where people dress a little better and brush off the crumbs, not eat them.

Easy Equations

DAing was made infinitely more aggravating by the personalities and peculiarities of all the bastards, uh make that first-class human beings, you had to serve. All of whom, naturally, expected undivided attention. DAs, even those not good at math, soon learned that they must deal far too many times with two equations:

Anchor = ego.
Ego = prick.

In pre-computer days anyone writing a radio newscast at CBS News was brought rolls of wire copy from AP, Reuters and UPI, and the DAs were expected to remember that one anchor liked her copy rolled so the latest stuff was first while another anchor on the same shift demanded that his rolls start with the oldest news first.

One anchor might want a ruler and a red grease pencil at his desk along with the rolled copy, and if the DAs could find only black grease pencils that day he would sulk for most of his shift. The guy's making $150,000 a year—in 1984 for God's sakes—and he's pouting. Yes, it is possible to have a wonderful, powerful voice and not a scintilla of common sense.

Copy editors, assignment editors and writers also had their own whims about how copy should be rolled and what tools should be waiting for them. While it was not part of the normal office supplies, one veteran CBS editor kept a brick near her for use as a paperweight for desk notes and memos. In my days as a writer, I would sometimes hide the brick if I saw she wasn't looking or had left her desk. She would never say anything about it, pretending to go about her duties as she glanced around the newsroom for her brick. While I agree that was childish, if newsrooms only hired the fully mature they would be severely short-handed.

Being the lowest of the low, DAs were easy to pick on when things went wrong. The wrong tape was played on the air? Blame it on the DA who took the tapes into the studio. The anchor stumbled when reading the stock market figures? Blame it on the DA who scribbled the numbers down after phoning the New York Stock Exchange. The anchor mispronounced the name of a Wyoming town where three miners were trapped? Blame it on the DA who called to find out how to say it.

After a messed up newscast, the most commonly heard sentence began with an anchor, editor, technician or desk assistant saying, "I thought you said…." A lack of clear communication in the communications business was not unheard of.

In a stunning advance for civilization, the young folks doing all these tasks at CBS News have now had the title of desk associate bestowed upon them, making a smoother transition for those who decide they hate news, newsrooms and newspeople and want to sign on with Macy's as sales associates.

Through the years I learned a lot from desk assistants. Les Blatt, a DA at ABC Radio, introduced this small-town Hoosier to scrambled eggs on a hard roll and the movies of Jean-Luc Godard. (These were separate learning experiences.) Another ABC desk assistant asked me to read an early draft of his book. Although I knew nothing about how a book should be put together and probably still don't, Larry Hughes's effort, "You Can See A Lot Standing Under A Flare In The Republic Of Vietnam: My Year at War," was published by William Morrow. And it was an ex-CBS DA who gave the first valid reason I ever heard for trying to get into law school: "To defend you, McCoy, from all the discrimination suits." Myra Michael was accepted, passed the bar exam and is now an administrative law judge in New York City.

Then there is Jack McDonald who, not long after leaving CBS News, utilized his phone expertise to talk to the mother of Marla Maples about why he wanted to take her daughter to the annual White House Correspondents' Association dinner. This was after Marla had been seen with The Donald (as in Trump) and before she told him "I do" or whatever she said. As Jack privately tells the story (the guy doesn't have even a sliver of braggart genes), he kept assuring the mother his intentions were entirely honorable. It paid off.

I was in my office when I came to the Style section of *The Washington Post* and saw two pictures of Mr. McDonald and Ms. Maples—he in a tux, she in a fine evening gown. In seconds I was on the phone screaming, affectionately, "You son of a bitch. You God damn son of a bitch. Way to go. Way to go!" I may never have been so proud of someone I had worked with. It was comic book hero stuff. What NERVE, what a feat of DARING!

I also remember a young man on an elevator at ABC News on a Friday, pay day. We had both been down to see the cashier, and on the ride up the DA, who had just started at the network, said, with disappointment in his voice, "I thought I would get paid today." I asked if he had any money. "Yes," he replied. "Don't lie to me," I said, imitating an adult. He admitted he didn't have much, and I gave him $50 until he got paid. It may not sound like much now, but you could have a pretty decent weekend in New York in the mid '60s with $50. At least you could eat.

I often had a very short fuse when dealing with DAs and probably was incredibly rude many times without realizing it. Maybe a few of them will see this and change their minds about me. Probably not. If they do read it, they'll probably say, "So he was nice, once, to one kid. What does he want, a medal?"

Well, no, but I am glad my grandkids never saw me in my bellowing mode in a newsroom when I was convinced I was the only one who knew anything.

9

"Stand Up so We Can See Your Tits."

*A*lthough my wife, Irene, has never worked in a newsroom, I've often told other journalists that she asks the best questions. If an important aspect of a story isn't addressed in a newscast, she will immediately pinpoint it and ask, "Well, how about...?"

In the paper one morning I read that Vinny Testaverde, a forty-three-year-old quarterback, had been signed by the New England Patriots when the NFL season was nearly half over. "Vinny Testaverde is coming back," I told Irene. "The Patriots signed him."

"To do what?" she demanded.

The answer for the rest of that season was basically nothing, except stand on the sidelines in a nice, clean uniform. (A year later Testaverde signed another contract, this time with the Carolina Panthers, and did get his uniform dirty, a few times.)

Based on nothing except my own experience, I think women journalists have their own approach to finding out the news and may ask better questions than men. They certainly ask different questions.

After a long time on the disabled list during the 2006 baseball season, Gary Sheffield, then the star right fielder for the New York Yankees, was put back into the lineup but at first base. A superb athlete, Sheffield was having problems making the adjustment on defense and at times was more of a liability than an asset. He was bobbling catches and didn't always sense where a first baseman should position himself or what to do in certain situations.

In the midst of this turmoil, Kimberly Jones of the YES Network asked Sheffield, "When's the last time in your athletic career you have felt like this?" Is that a terrific question? A male reporter, I submit, would have asked a more specific and less humanizing question, something along the lines of "what's the hardest thing you've had to learn in moving from right field to first base?" That probably would have elicited some jock mumbo jumbo along the lines of the ever popular "I've just got to step it up a notch."

The lady reporter's question was a polite way of asking a proud, talented man about the embarrassment he was experiencing. "When's the last time in your athletic career you have felt like this?" drew a simple, understandable one word response: "Never."

It was the retirement of Larry Bird that convinced me that women journalists think differently than the men in their midst. In August of 1992, Bird had scheduled a news conference to talk about his future, and, while all the speculation pointed to a decision by the Boston Celtics' legend to retire, CBS Radio hadn't found anyone—coach, player, executive or top sports writer—able or willing to confirm it.

Thanks to the smarts of a woman editor, Kay Lazar, the CBS newscast at noon led with word of Bird's retirement plans. Who confirmed it? His mother. Kay called Georgia Bird, and she said yes, it's true. Larry's retiring. The CBS newsroom was packed with guys, and there wasn't a one of us—certainly not me, a basketball fanatic—who would have ever thought of calling someone's mother and asking her to tell us what her son was going to do before he got around to telling the rest of the country.

I've never stopped thanking Kay or retelling that story. Women are listened to in newsrooms now. They're taken seriously. That hasn't always been the case, especially when there weren't many of them in news and almost none were bosses. (Yes, despite the masculine acronym, we are now at a stage where a Jane can be a TOM. Ah, equality.)

During my early days in journalism, John F. Kennedy was president, and there were few newswomen at UPI in Chicago. (Kennedy wasn't to blame. I simply like associating his name with a shortage of women, probably one of the few times that's been done.) While on the overnight shift for many months at UPI's National Radio desk, I don't recall any women working alongside me all the time. Whether this was reverse discrimination, I don't know.

One lady Unipresser I do recall vividly is someone we will call Darleen, a charter member of the don't-give-me-any-shit school, who seemed to have a cigarette permanently attached, barely, to her lower lip. She was in charge of the TTS wire, a service that enabled newspapers to justify and set type on UPI copy sent to them.

On weekday afternoons there was a half hour overlap between the day and the evening shifts and finding a place to sit was difficult. Darleen was irked by all the people, some of them standing, suddenly crowding around her. "There are more asses than seats," she loved to observe.

I believe Darleen was still at UPI in Chicago fussing about that when I left for ABC News in the mid '60s. I don't think there were any women working regularly then as writers, editors or anchors at ABC's radio operation in New York.

There were also precious few women writers in the Central Newsroom of RFE in Munich, my next major stop after ABC. RFE did have several German women teletype operators, and very good ones, who were given copy in English to type on the wire that went to the Polish, Czechoslovak, Hungarian, Romanian and Bulgarian newsrooms.

By 1971 I was back in New York, this time at CBS News, Radio where all the editors were men except one. Again I spent many hours on the always entertaining overnight where, without question, one woman writer was the object of well-deserved verbal abuse, much of it initiated by me. She was a talker. Ceaseless, non-stop, never-ending, on and on. She even thought her trips to the can were of interest and would announce to the entire newsroom that she was headed to "the facilities."

You could be busy with a piece of tape or editing copy for a newscast minutes away, and she would begin a long, involved, in-group, complex, boring, preposterous story. Despite all evidence, she apparently assumed people wanted to hear this stuff. If I got trapped by her at the start of one of these epics, I would turn to anyone else unlucky enough to be in the room or studio and say, "I'm sorry" — and damn it, I was sorry for them — "can you listen to this, please? I have work to do" and then leave. She never learned and kept going on and on, midnight to eight a.m., ceaseless, non-stop, never-ending.

To deal with this torture, another writer and I devised a ploy where we would throw out a word at her that had something to do with what's between your legs and watch what happened.

"'Smegma,' now there's a word worth knowing," one of us would say with a smirk and walk away.

There would soon be a scream. Pearl, our made-up name for her, had gone to the dictionary and looked up "smegma." I remember that "merkin" — as in the sentence "Gee, Aunt Betty, is that a new merkin you're wearing?" — also produced loud Pearl shrieks from the dictionary area. If you are unfamiliar with these words, it will be a joy to look them up and perhaps identify with Pearl's screams.

Yes, indeed this was the behavior of twelve-year olds, but let me toss a question your way: have you ever worked the overnight for a long period of time (less than four months doesn't count) and been forced to share time and space with a babbling machine? If you haven't, you're welcome to keep your opinions to yourself. If this had been a man, we would have told him straight off that he was full of shit and to put a sock on it.

During my first go around at CBS, I don't remember any woman regularly anchoring hourly newscasts, at least not from New York. When I returned in 1980, Stephanie Shelton was anchoring and reporting. She covered Ronald Reagan's winning campaign for the White House. I spent a month or so traveling with her as a producer. We're still on speaking terms, so apparently I behaved myself both on and off the job.

Not only were there more women in the CBS Radio newsroom in 1980, two of them were managers. When I moved over to television as assistant bureau manager, my boss was a woman, a first for me. She recalled that after getting in the door at CBS News with a low-level job she was interviewed for an opening with a lot more responsibility, and a well-known television producer asked her to "stand up so we can see your tits." She did, he did, and she got the job.

By the time I heard the story she was telling it with a smile. Whether there was intense anger beneath the smile, I don't know. She had shown that producer and probably other males sharing similar sentiments that she had talents above and beyond her knockers. She had done well and had been promoted.

Journalism can be a long, tedious string of weird hours, and women frequently faced many more obstacles in doing that than men. Single mothers, in particular, usually set limits on what shifts they could work. They couldn't go bouncing around the schedule—early mornings one week and late evening the next—as some young men, unmarried or married, could and did. Women managers joined in griping at times about the restrictions a woman editor or producer placed on her availability.

"Stacy is so inflexible," a lady TOM, struggling to complete a schedule would say.

Despite the many possibilities for complications and distractions, several of the best producers and editors at CBS Radio News were women with children—some single, others with very supportive husbands who accepted, apparently, that at three in the morning their bed was going to be empty.

If the babysitter got sick or quit on short notice that used to present a dilemma for a woman due in a newsroom in two hours. By the time I left journalism in 2006, it was not unheard of for daddies in the news business to stay home when there was a problem, allowing the mommies to go to their jobs in another newsroom or at a bank. That would have never happened when I started out nearly a half century ago.

Peggy Noonan, now a big time political writer-analyst, was on the CBS News, Radio payroll for a number of years, and her duties included writing Dan Rather's daily commentary. Having no idea of Noonan's political leanings, I was probably the most surprised person in the newsroom when she left CBS for a job at the Reagan White House. Only then did I understand her frosty reaction to something I had said not long after the death of a famous movie star.

Noonan had asked the newsroom in general, "Does anyone know where you can get a good cold hero?" My immediate response: "Yeah. Try John Wayne." Not a bad wisecrack for my money, and it got a big laugh at the expense of the late Mr. Wayne, a favorite of conservatives.

Noonan wasn't amused. She stared for a long time at me. It was as if I had called her Margaret, her given name. Although we are far apart on politics, I think Noonan is an exceptional writer, particularly on deadline. (Peggy wasn't the one suspended when Rather messed up the lyrics to "The Gambler.")

Judd, Muller and Potter—No, Not a Law Firm

Women anchors and reporters with ambitions to get into television are still generally judged by a harsher standard than men. A man with average looks and decent broadcast skills has an easier time of finding on air work in TV than an equally-qualified woman who isn't knock down gorgeous.

At CBS News, Jackie Judd, Judy Muller, and Deborah Potter were three of the finest writers and anchors there, but apparently because none of them was considered a beauty queen and all were older than twenty-four, the TOMs of CBS unwisely formed a perception that they weren't "television." Their journalism expertise and broadcasting talents heard every day on radio didn't mean bubkes at CBS-TV news. Intelligent ladies all, Judd, Muller and Potter went elsewhere to do steady TV work and did very well—Judd and Muller at ABC News and Potter at CNN. The TOMs at CBS News, a clique that included a few women, must have seen the three ladies working for the competition, and I wonder if they ever second-guessed themselves.

Although there's probably no connection, it's worth noting that the network that wouldn't put Jackie, Judy and Deborah on television regularly named a woman with almost no journalism background, former Congresswoman Susan Molinari, co-anchor of the Saturday morning TV news. The assumption seemed to have been that if you were real perky while being interviewed on television, as Molinari had been when a member of Congress, you would naturally be real perky if you were doing the interviewing. Well, it turned out that wasn't true. In this case, the TOMs may have forgotten a truism often voiced in their own shop, "Assumption is the mother of fuck up."

I admit having to fight against making an instant judgment when

I see for the first time a new attractive woman reporter or anchor on TV. There are so many dumb, unqualified but beautiful women doing television "news" that when a very good-looking lady with smarts appears on the screen I have trouble immediately accepting her as a journalist. I concede that's a personal failure of an aging white male, one of only 3,476 that I am aware of and am working on.

10

"Do We Have Anybody in Budapest?"

> "It's all up to you, a one-person band, in a
> do-or-die kind of thing."
> — Bill Gasperini, veteran stringer

Of all the get-rich-quick schemes ever devised, radio stringer has to be high on the list. (There's that sarcasm again.) Though absolutely vital to a respectable news operation, overseas stringers or freelancers were consistently underappreciated, starting with the money they made — less than $50 for a report or piece of sound on a CBS newscast. That rate has inched up only a couple of bucks in the sixteen years since I left CBS. It was unbelievable then and even more so now.

Usually a stringer had no company benefits, no one nearby to help with technical problems, and in many countries it could take an hour or more to get a phone call through to the New York desk where the chances were high you would be told the line was bad and could you call back. When a second call did get through, the chances could be even higher that the desk wasn't all that hot about the story you pitched earlier because something newer and better had come along.

Adding to the challenge, a commercial radio network's appetite for international news was often limited to the spectacular: plane crashes, earthquakes, coups, rioting, or an incident involving Americans or the U.S. government. (Straining to emphasize an American angle to a story was a bad habit at U.S. networks that could at times distort or completely miss the import of what had taken place.)

Looking for stringers was one of the most difficult, time-consuming tasks during my days as a TOM at CBS Radio. Many freelancers were young with very little experience in either print or broadcasting and sounded stiff and dull when reading their copy. The writers working in tape rooms frequently didn't have the time, or maybe the temperament or expertise, to coach a novice on developing a more polished and relaxed broadcast style, both in delivery and word choice. I tried to help stringers sound better and more relaxed, but I could have done more. I did make sure pieces from new voices were fed to stations on an affiliate service called Newsfeed, telling writers and editors, "If they don't make some money from us now, they're not going to be available when we really need them." (Newsfeed paid the magnificent sum of $25.) Things weren't helped when a stringer offered a piece of marginal interest at a busy time in the newsroom. Many stringers faced the same dilemma as young baseball players: how were they going to get any better if they didn't play every day.

TOMs could be embarrassingly ignorant of how precious money was to freelancers. A stringer in Latin America did a live interview on a breaking story one afternoon with WCBS-TV, the network's flagship station in New York. Several weeks later he told me he had never been paid, and I called the WCBS-TV news director to relay the message. "Oh, we don't pay for things like that. It's professional courtesy," he said. After trying several approaches and getting the same "professional courtesy" nonsense, I realized I was talking to a nincompoop with no concept of freelancing or how urgently a stringer could need money to keep going. They didn't have the luxury of giving their work away. The news director had forgotten, if he ever knew, what a difference $100 could make in someone's life. I'm pretty sure we dipped into the radio budget to make up for WCBS-TV's refusal to pay the stringer a dime.

Meager fees didn't mean stringers were immune to the normal tug of war between editor and reporter and, at times, unreasonable demands. Some editors would insist that a stringer head immediately to the scene of a breaking story. The stringer in turn was often reluctant to leave his home or office for valid reasons. It could take a long time in chaotic traffic to get near the site of the action and being there, in the days of less than instant mobile communications, left him with no way to monitor or record local radio and TV for updated information and official announcements. If he had stayed put, he could make phone calls, tape interviews and the output of radio and TV and perhaps keep an eye on a local wire service. As a solo act—"a one-person band" in the words of long-time stringer Bill Gasperini—he was in a much better position to know the major elements of the story if he stayed in his home or office. Being at the scene meant being out of pocket and out of touch, costing him money because he wouldn't know as much nor be able to file as often.

Another difficulty a stringer (or even a CBS News staff reporter) could face was doing a piece on a story a New York editor or producer had spotted in *The New York Times*. There could be a problem if what was filed strayed too much from what was in *The Times*. That had to be frustrating for a stringer, confident that his research and interviews resulted in an accurate if somewhat different story than the one that attracted the attention of the New York editor. Who knows how much editing was done to the piece in *The Times*? What appeared in the paper could have been more the views and words of an editor in New York than the reporter in the field.

Stringers who had been overseas a long time could become so immersed in the culture of the country where they lived that they were out of sync with what interested an American audience. After Bing Crosby had a fatal heart attack at a golf course in Spain, CBS couldn't find its Madrid stringer. When the stringer finally called the New York desk, he hadn't written anything on Crosby but was offering something else of little consequence. A fuming CBS News editor, hungry for a report on the death of a major American entertainer, was told, "Oh, you want something on that? I thought he retired."

"Sprechen Sie Deutsch?"

One of the most irritating aspects of handling stringers was the out of the blue phone calls from strangers a day or sometimes just hours before a widely anticipated U.S. military action. "Hey, CBS, do you need some help in Panama?" Well, yes, you dimwit, we probably could have used an extra body if you'd called a couple of weeks ago, giving us time to check you out to see if you are a journalist or a loose cannon posing as one.

A few stringers did spectacular work despite making what I considered an odd phone call at the start. Jesse Schulman was guilty on both counts. He called and asked if we had a stringer in West Germany. My immediate reply was, "Do you speak German?"

"No," Jesse said, "but I can learn. My girlfriend is German." Right, I thought, a big shot! Not long afterwards—Jesse thinks it was no longer than two months—he called again, saying he knew German and was ready to go. And go he did, covering the fall of the Berlin Wall and the turmoil that preceded it and the first Iraq war. As often happened once a competent radio stringer made his or her presence known, television news gave Jesse much needed work and money as a producer.

After Jesse's reporting on Desert Storm impressed the television side, he was offered a job as a staff reporter in Jerusalem. He was part of the CBS News team that won a Peabody and two Emmys for coverage of the assassination of Israeli Prime Minister Yitzhak Rabin. Perhaps I wouldn't have thought Jesse was just blowing hot air in that first phone conversation if I had known that he had a PhD in neurosciences. Imagine that—a PhD who wanted to work as a radio stringer calling the executive editor of CBS Radio News who was so bright he had to go to summer class in high school to finish a shop project, a very lopsided table lamp.

Kimberly Dozier was another talented journalist who went from radio stringer to reporting for CBS television news. After freelancing in Cairo for print outlets and CBS Radio, she took over the top radio news job in London, a post that came with a salary and benefits and that required a first-rate journalist capable of keeping up with twenty-seven things at once in the United Kingdom as well as parts of the Middle East, Europe and Africa, where stringers were hard to find. It was firefighter duty, focusing on one hot spot after another. As Kimberly recalled, one day you might be covering Princess Diana, the next day the Spice Girls, the day after that a bombing in Northern Ireland and then be sent to Kosovo to report on the latest trouble there. The London person also provided the New York desk with tape of the generally excellent coverage from BBC reporters in volatile, neglected parts of the world.

After London, it was on to Jerusalem for Kimberly to report for both WCBS-TV and Newspath, a service for CBS TV affiliates. Later, promoted to the rank of a CBS News correspondent, she spent much of her time, nearly three years, reporting on the war in Iraq for the CBS Evening News With Dan Rather and other broadcasts. On a street in Baghdad in 2006, she was critically injured by a bomb that killed four others—her cameraman, soundman, a U.S. soldier and an Iraqi interpreter. After many operations and a long recovery, she was assigned to the CBS Washington bureau, focusing on national security matters. Kimberly had wanted to return to her old beat, but there were TOMs at CBS who resisted this, apparently thinking she might not be able to handle it. She left the network for The Associated Press where she was the Intelligence Writer, tracking and finding stories about the CIA, the Pentagon and other agencies. From the AP she moved on to The Daily Beast, a website that boasts it does "award-winning original reporting."

Before there was Kimberly in London, there was Adam, Adam Raphael. A Brit who had lived in the States, he sounded like an American on CBS but, I'm told, like a proper Englishman when reading copy for the BBC, a previous employer. He was a delightful person, good at and devoted to meaningful reportage and the writing of interesting letters, both private and public—his Letter From London series for CBS News won a citation for excellence from the Overseas Press Club of America.

Although Adam had a wonderful sense of humor, his years in the U.S. didn't always protect him from misreading American wisecracks. In Poland during a visit by John Paul II, Adam asked the desk how long a piece was wanted for the next broadcast. A busy copy editor joked, "two-and-one-half minutes." That would have left thirty seconds for all other news in the opening section of the newscast. Adam started writing and filed what was requested, a piece two-and-one-half minutes long. When the copy editor discovered this, he raced back to the studio and managed to chop this extravaganza down to a more reasonable length. According to CBS folklore, from then on this editor went easy on the sarcasm when he knew Adam might hear him.

Ed Bradley is often portrayed as a journalist who was "able to leap tall buildings in a single bound," catapulting from the lowly status of a stringer in Paris to the ranks of a CBS News correspondent and a mainstay on "60 Minutes." While the tall buildings part is true, it shouldn't be forgotten that Bradley spent about four years inside the CBS family as a reporter for WCBS Radio in New York before freelancing in Paris.

For a brief, marvelous time, the radio budget contained money for contracts for a few reporters overseas in addition to the one in London. Ronnie Hess, a writer for radio in New York and fluent in French, went to Paris with a contract. A listing of a few of the stories Ronnie covered from 1984 to 1987, many of them outside France, shows how dependent CBS News, Radio was on stringers and contract reporters:

Normandy, '84 (Fortieth anniversary of D-Day)
Syria, '85 (TWA hijacking, last hostages arrive there after a seventeen-day nightmare)
Germany, '85 (Reagan visit to Bergen-Belsen concentration camp)
Switzerland, '85 and Iceland '86 (Gorbachev-Reagan summits)
Sweden, '86 (Assassination of Swedish prime minister Palme)
Germany, '86 (American reporter Daniloff freed after being held by Soviets)
Poland, '87 (Pope Paul II visit)
France, '87 (Trial of Klaus Barbie, Gestapo chief in Lyons)

The funds for this sort of essential coverage became scarce after the CBS Corporation was put in the hands of investor Laurence Tisch. Ronnie, not wanting to face the uncertain financial future of an ordinary stringer, returned to the States to work again as a writer in network radio news. In all the pieces she filed, I believe my only criticism was an occasional reminder to pronounce the names of French newspapers like an ordinary American not the Parisians she dealt with every day, so little old Larry McCoy and other U.S. listeners would know what she was saying.

"If All You're Going to Do Is Yell at Me, I'll Hang Up."

CBS Radio paid a lot of attention to news from the Middle East as did many of its listeners. I took more angry phone calls complaining about something said about Israel or the Palestinians than on any other subject. I would tell an agitated caller, "We can have a conversation on this, but if all you're going to do is yell at me, I'll hang up." That frequently did the trick. When it didn't, I hung up. Callers accused CBS News of not reporting the truth, of siding with the Palestinians against the Israelis. A common argument was that Palestinians were terrorists and should be labeled as such in our broadcasts.

I said out loud more than once that it seemed there wasn't anything in the Middle East CBS News, Radio wouldn't report. I remember shaking my head in the '90s when a New York anchor told listeners that Jordan's rubber-stamp parliament had passed a resolution criticizing the U.S. Wow! It would have been news if it hadn't passed. Other times CBS could be criticized for appearing to play down stories that made Israel look bad. In the winter of 1994, an Israeli settler opened fire in a mosque, killing about thirty Muslims and wounding more than a hundred. CBS reported it on newscasts but didn't make a big deal out of it by doing Updates at thirty-one past the hour. It was obviously the best story of the morning. After a call to the desk by me and probably a medley of expletives, the newsroom began doing Updates.

Most of the time CBS News had two journalists in Israel looking out for radio's interests plus a TV correspondent. One of the radio people had a contract guaranteeing an annual salary, the other was a stringer who covered weekends and helped out on big stories. During a long stretch when I was in charge of freelancers, Lawrence Rifkin was the guy with the salary. Robert Berger became the weekend duty person for radio in 1989 and, despite his stringer status, ended up with a pretty good deal I thought, being sent all over—Macedonia, Bosnia, Egypt, Bahrain, Jordan, Kenya, India, Pakistan, Indonesia, Haiti and trips to hot spots on board U.S. Navy ships.

Shortly after he set foot in Macedonia (his first trip outside Israel for CBS News), my phone rang. Robert had been promised a satellite phone to assure high audio quality for the reports and tape he would be filing. Bobby, as I like to call him, was apparently unaware that a satellite phone came in two heavy silver suitcases and had to be assembled. He asked me what to do. Always a patient and understanding TOM, my answer was two-fold: figure it out yourself and leave me alone. It shouldn't be forgotten that Dale Carnegie never worked in radio news because if he had he wouldn't have written that silly book about winning friends and influencing people.

Jim Rupert remembers a different, warmer approach when Joe Dembo was in charge of stringers. After serving in the Peace Corps in Morocco, Jim filed a few pieces from there and from Tunisia for CBS Radio. Jim says it wasn't until years later, as an editor on *The Washington Post*'s foreign desk, that he "fully appreciated the rarity of Joe's patience and attentiveness to an unknown kid halfway around the world." Jim tried to show the same patience and concern every chance he could in helping an energetic stringer reshape a piece for *The Post*. Jim believes those he helped "owe Joe a debt of gratitude too."

Jim had signed on with *The Washington Post* after CBS, covering the Soviet-Afghan war for the paper. Fifteen years with *The Post* were followed by seven with *Newsday* and then four years as the South Asia political reporter for Bloomberg News. Not bad at all.

CBS News, Radio had two capable stringers in Moscow during the upheaval that led to the disintegration of the Soviet Union and the later uprising against Russian President Boris Yeltsin in which tanks fired on the parliament building controlled by opposition forces. Terry Phillips, one of the stringers, was staying in a hotel where government troops backing Yeltsin had set up a command post. He shared a telephone with the Yeltsin loyalists, with the military using it to pass along orders and Terry taking it to file for CBS News. When shooting started, all hands took cover behind furniture. One day after gunfire sprayed through a window, a soldier on the floor with Terry handed him a spent round and asked, "Souvenir?" He still has it.

During those long days of turmoil and gunfire, I kept assuring Terry and Bill Gasperini, the other stringer, that there was plenty of work for both of them. In addition to their reports for radio, they did pieces for CBS television news. Bill, who began stringing for CBS from Central America, says, "The collapse of the Soviet Union" was a "story so huge it became all-consuming but also led to opportunities in the feature world, such as documentary TV reports and films" for other companies besides CBS.

When Terry returned to the States, he had a job with CBS Newspath in Detroit. Bill relocated to the Boston area but in a way never left Russia. The last I heard he was an online editor for RIA Novosti, a Russian news agency.

Freelancers sent on an assignment away from home normally had their airfare, hotel, ground transportation and phone bills paid along with meal money and a day rate of around $350. That rate paid for all the pieces a stringer filed on a given day, be it eight or thirty-eight. If a stringer was asked to go where there was fighting or the likelihood of violence, I tried to remember to alert the personnel department to make sure insurance coverage kicked in.

I went to bat for stringers over expenses and fees, though once or twice someone ignored my warnings about checking with me before going somewhere and running up hotel and meal bills. When this happened, my limited supply of patience was quickly exhausted, resulting in yelling and slammed phones. (No, Maggy Sterner, I'm not talking about you.)

Missing in Iraq

News organizations need reporters, photographers and videographers willing to head into war zones and areas in turmoil to find out what's happening. Governments and opposition forces can't be trusted to tell the truth, so it's imperative that objective journalists see and record what is going on and talk to those involved, both combatants and civilians if possible. During a brief stay as a TV producer in El Salvador, I never saw even a skirmish in the civil war, yet I was very uneasy; every male over fourteen seemed to have a large gun. A foreign editor at CBS News always said you never asked a reporter or a crew to do something you wouldn't do. There might be a potential assignment that was simply too dangerous.

A few young freelancers — eager to get noticed, to see the action first-hand, and perhaps to make a few bucks — put themselves in harm's way, guessing correctly that their material would be aired or published by major networks or newspapers. Not all of those decisions ended well.

After Operation Desert Storm drove Iraqi forces out of Kuwait, stringer Frank Smyth called from Syria to say that he and two photographers — one a German-born Romanian, the other French-Vietnamese — were planning to cross into northern Iraq where Kurdish forces were fighting against Saddam Hussein. I asked Frank if any of the three spoke a language that would be useful if they ran into problems in Iraq. When the answer was "no," I said it didn't strike me as the best idea I had ever heard.

Frank filed a few times from inside Iraq for radio and also sent footage shown on CBS-TV news. Then silence. He and the photographers, Gad Gross and Alain Buu, had disappeared. Over the next three weeks, producer Carol Gillesberg and I along with representatives from the photographers' agencies tried to find them, talking to other journalists who had been in the Kirkuk area of Iraq about the same time, checking over and over with U.S. and U.N. agencies, the Red Cross and the Committee to Protect Journalists. Nothing. We couldn't make contact with anyone who knew anything.

An uncle of Frank's called me at home one night extremely upset, charging that CBS News wasn't doing enough. I assured him I cared and was doing little else at work but looking for his nephew. From time to time, both CBS radio and television news ran a few lines in newscasts about the missing American reporter and the photographers. We hoped this might remind U.S. government officials and others that there was unfinished business to take care of.

Smyth and Buu had been captured by Iraqi troops in Kirkuk, the Kurdish capital, were questioned and eventually taken to a prison in Baghdad. Gad Gross and Bakhtiar, an armed Kurdish guerrilla serving as a translator-guide, were killed. One afternoon a desk assistant walked into my office and asked, "Do you want to talk to Frank Smyth?" I went running for the phone. Allowed to make a call from Baghdad, Frank was guarded in what he said, lying when asked what had happened to Gross. A quick special report was done about the release of Smyth and Buu. After arriving in Jordan, where Frank could talk freely, we did another special.

Frank is now the Senior Adviser for Journalist Security for the Committee to Protect Journalists. Among the items on the CPJ's website is the "Journalist Security Guide, Covering The News In A Dangerous And Changing World." Frank wrote it.

"Those Were My Golden Years."

There could be fireworks when a stringer came up with information at odds with what a CBS News correspondent had been told. Scott Wallace, stringing from San Salvador, called minutes before a newscast to say rebel forces had surrounded a luxury hotel in the city. That didn't jibe with what a Washington correspondent was about to report from his sources—that all was well and the rebels had surrendered. The editor, Kit Borgman, and the anchor, Vicki Kelley, decided they would begin the broadcast by saying there were conflicting reports about the incident and lead with the stringer and then go to the Washington correspondent.

A vice president was soon in the newsroom, demanding to know why a broadcast would air a report from a stringer that contradicted what a correspondent in Washington had learned. Well, duh. One of them was on the scene and saw what was going on. The other one wasn't. And yes, Scott Wallace was right.

In looking for stringers, I frequently called a U. S. embassy press office or a print reporter, asking that they spread the word that CBS Radio was looking for help. Sometimes I didn't have to do anything.

Women journalists married to print reporters contacted me when their husbands were reassigned. Katherine Arms began stringing for CBS News, Radio in Cyprus where her husband, a Reuters reporter, was based. One of her first stories was the hijacking of a Kuwaiti Airways jet to Cyprus, a drama that went on for days. Katherine started the glamorous life of a radio stringer by sleeping under a table and filing a report nearly every hour on the hour.

Katherine went on to file for CBS from Beirut during the Lebanese civil war, from Jordan during the first Gulf War and later Africa, operating out of Kenya. While she was in Beirut, she would alert me when she planned to go to a troubled area of the country. Not to worry, she would say, "I'm a woman and that means I'm unimportant in an Arab culture. I'll be okay." She was and says she was always treated with respect.

Maggy Sterner was a fine stringer for CBS Radio in Manila for three-and-a-half years, covering earthquakes, volcanic eruptions and politics, and another three-and-a-half years in Johannesburg where she concentrated on the first democratic votes by blacks in South Africa, the inauguration of the country's first black president and the transition from a minority-ruled nation to a majority-ruled one. Maggy also reported on the "miscellaneous and sundry shenanigans and hijinks by various and sundry characters in both places."

Among the other good stringers I worked with: Adrienne Bard in Mexico City; Elaine Cobbe who split her time in Paris among CBS News, non-American broadcast outlets and the *Irish Independent* newspaper and who did several reporting stints outside of France; Peter Maass who reported from Seoul for CBS News before moving to Europe where he covered the Bosnia war for *The Washington Post* and later wrote books about that and about oil plus articles for The New Yorker, *The New York Times* and others; Ann Mustard who reported from Moscow, Istanbul and Vienna where her husband headed the agricultural section at U.S. diplomatic outposts; Margaret "Penny" Rogg who worked as a CBS stringer in Beirut and Cyprus before becoming a reporter-producer in Cairo; and Mary Wisniewski, married to a wire service reporter, who filed from Moscow and Warsaw, her first look at the Polish capital coinciding with the start of a strike that led to the formation of the Solidarity movement. Both Bard and Cobbe still file for CBS News.

I never did very well lining up stringers in most of Eastern Europe or Africa. If an editor asked, "Do we have anyone in Budapest?" or Brazzaville, the answer was probably "nope." The newsroom could only hope that a compelling story in Hungary or Congo was being covered by a BBC reporter or that CBS could track down a newspaper reporter in the country willing to be interviewed.

With little money, long hours, few compliments, and a status equivalent to a hubcap, why did anyone want to be a stringer? Because they cared about what was going on in the world, were curious and courageous and thrived on the exhilaration that came from facing deadline after deadline. Here's what some of them say:

"It IS cool all the places I've gotten to go." –Robert Berger

"I had some of my best and favorite adventures working for CBS radio." –Maggy Sterner

"…it didn't matter so much that the money was bad when the assignment was good, when the story was worth covering…." –Elaine Cobbe

"All in all, I really enjoyed my time at CBS…Being a radio reporter was undoubtedly the best job I ever had – EVER." –Terry Phillips

"…an amazing twenty-year reporting run around the world that took me to 'stories' on six continents." –Bill Gasperini

"When the whole thing was over, you called me and said, '…you really saved our bacon out there.' That was the nicest thing anyone had ever said to me, or so it seemed at the time." –Katherine Arms

"It was such a badge of honor to work for CBS Radio." –Penny Rogg

"I phoned in to the news desk on my wedding night. It was that kind of life, and I loved it…those were my golden years." –Jesse Schulman (Jesse married that girlfriend who taught him German.)

11

"You'll Never Work for CBS Radio Again."

A newspaper reporter called CBS one day to talk about Brian Andrews, a stringer in Atlanta. He does a good job, I immediately told the reporter from *The Atlanta Journal*. The conversation went back and forth about Brian's talents and hustle before this question, "Are you aware Brian Andrews is fifteen-years-old?"

To say there was a long pause on my end of the line would be quite accurate. After regaining the power of speech, I "finally blurted" — in the words of the newspaper account — that I didn't know Brian's age, nor that he was still in high school. It made a good story, local teen filing news reports for a top U.S. network. Brian apparently came home from school, checked out what was going on around Atlanta, called an official or eyewitness for a taped interview and then wrote a spot and sent it to CBS. One editor suggested a check of the desk logs would show a pattern of when Brian offered pieces, almost always in the afternoon after school. He did solid stories, as I told the newspaper, and he sure didn't sound like a teenager.

With my focus on stringers abroad, I paid little attention to free-lancers in the States but after hanging up with the newspaper reporter I called Andrews. More than a quarter of a century later he remembers me screaming, "You'll never work for CBS Radio again." Way to go, Mr. Executive Editor! Standing tall, upholding CBS News standards, protecting American radio listeners from fifteen-year-olds. Some prophet I am. At this writing, Mr. Brian Andrews, forty-one years old, is an investigative reporter and anchor for WFOR-TV in Miami, a station owned by CBS.

Don't ask me why, but there was virtually no checking on the background of domestic stringers. If someone worked for an affiliate or offered acceptable material from a city where either there was no CBS affiliate or a weak one, he or she was welcomed by editors eager for fresh pieces. The CBS desk had never asked Brian where he worked or any other questions. At the time CBS either didn't have an affiliate in Atlanta or at least one that focused on news. Brian knew what he was doing, and if he called with a decent story he was asked to file it.

There was also an unusual stringer situation in St. Louis where CBS owned a powerhouse radio station, KMOX, which didn't cover much of what the network considered news. The network once reported, based on information from KMOX, that several people from Missouri were being held hostage in Eastern Europe—Poland, I believe. Trying to find out more, I called KMOX. "Well, we don't actually know they're being held hostage, but that's what we're saying on the air," a person in the newsroom relayed to me. Ah, I see. Close enough. As I recall the Missourians were delayed at the border because of a question about their visas but were soon cleared to head to their next destination. All "hostage" situations should end so quickly and smoothly.

KMOX radio was unhappy when CBS Radio aired pieces from a St. Louis TV reporter, John Mills. John was young (but definitely over fifteen), eager, competent, and he chased news. After a report by John was put on a newscast and KMOX called to protest, my response was that the newsroom thought the story was worth reporting, and if KMOX had covered it we wouldn't have put John on the air. I suspect it was an unsatisfactory conversation for both parties.

Many reporters from affiliates and the CBS owned and operated stations (O&Os) were eager to file for the network. It meant a little extra money and national exposure. Their contributions were invaluable in helping CBS News keep up on developments around the country and, frankly, filling all the air time in a twenty-four-hour-a-day operation. Not all God's children are equally gifted, and a few reporters had to be watched closely. A report that was considered okay at a local station might be rejected by a network editor or writer for reasons of fairness and/or clarity. A reporter for WCBS specializing in New York area crime stories had trouble distinguishing between fact and allegation, and often the network asked for rewrites to make the distinction clear.

Even good reporters have lapses. One O&O reporter whose work was usually top-notch referred to "a Polish concentration camp" in a piece aired on a CBS newscast. The network editor, tape room person and anchor should have caught this, and I told them so. When I pointed out to an editor at the O&O that it was a Nazi concentration camp and calling it a Polish one was not only inaccurate but very offensive to Poles, he seemed to think I was splitting hairs.

An affiliate reporter or two knew how to game the system, especially on slow news days. They would call Newsfeed, the service that provided pieces to affiliates, and file a strange story of limited interest at best. Frantic for anything to put on the next feed, the Newsfeed producer would include it because there was not much else around. One affiliate reporter was notorious for peddling second-rate stories nearly every damn day. CBS News managers and affiliates could complain all they wanted; the Newsfeed producer had to offer stations something on his feeds, and what was he to do when there didn't seem to be much happening?

The Preposition War

For years CBS News policy had been that only reporters employed by the news division could say "CBS News" in their sign offs. All others—stringers overseas and reporters at stations, including the CBS O&Os—had to use "**for** CBS News." A number of stringers, especially those filing from particularly risky spots of the world, thought having to clutter their sign offs with a preposition marked them as second-class citizens and lobbied for the right to drop it. Dispensation was seldom granted.

After the Westinghouse takeover of CBS, the new top TOMs in radio, one of them a long-time Westinghouse employee, saw no need for reporters from the O&Os to say "for." I opposed the change. The O&O reporters, as talented as they might be, didn't work for the news division but rather the radio division whose ranks included sales people, technicians, and former preppies in loafers who schmoozed station owners all day about the riches awaiting them as a CBS Radio affiliate. Reporters at CBS stations might do occasional anchor work that required them to read commercials, a no-no for network news people with the exception of Charles Osgood.

To an outsider this is probably a distinction without a difference. CBS was CBS. From the inside though, the lines were clearly drawn. As executive editor and later news director of CBS News, Radio, I was the boss of anchors and writers but not technicians. If a tech screwed up badly on a broadcast or showed up late on a very busy day, I couldn't bawl him out. I had to go to his boss and state my case.

I was dispatched to a meeting of top TV news executives and producers to argue both sides of the preposition case, a clear sign that the fix was in, that the new TOMs of radio had already made a decision. The meeting was merely a venue for the TV TOMs to announce they had no objections to radio dropping the "for," but the old rules would apply to stringers filing for television. These days some radio stringers granted exemption from using the preposition "for" are at times identified to listeners as CBS News "correspondents," elevating a freelance newsman to the vocabulary equivalent of the anchor of the CBS Evening News. I understand CBS News, Television has no standard policy on sign offs. In other words, you can say whatever you want on the air, which seems to be in keeping with the sharp decline in the respect for precision in language and for the difference between journalism and marketing. Calling a stringer a correspondent doesn't cost a dime and who is going to spot the exaggeration besides others in the news business?

After my phone call to the ex-kid stringer in Atlanta, it was years before he filed for CBS Radio again. Brian Andrews was upset and offended by my call and my manners back in 1988 but says "you lit a fire under me to keep me going" to become what he wanted to be, a radio reporter. When I talked to him in the summer of 2013, he was still filing from time to time for CBS Radio while working for the CBS-owned TV station in Miami. He doesn't seem to hold a grudge. I'm pretty sure I would. I probably should send him a free copy of this book. Nah. Maybe just email him this chapter. I don't want him to think I'm getting soft in my old age.

12

Werking Like ein Hund in Deutschland

The best newsroom I ever worked in was the Central Newsroom at Radio Free Europe in Munich. Journalists from the U.S., Australia, the U.K., Canada, New Zealand and Germany wrote the major international news stories of the day in English, and their copy was sent on an in-house wire service to the Romanian, Polish, Czechoslovak, Hungarian and Bulgarian news desks where it was translated for use in news programs.

As a general rule, these desks couldn't use anything on a newscast that hadn't come through Central News. As I understood it, this was a way of insuring that newscasts contained genuine news rather than the personal opinions of a Bulgarian exile who might think it was okay to tell listeners that the First Secretary of the Bulgarian Communist Party came from a long line of horse thieves and bed-wetters.

It was the toughest job I ever had and the most rewarding. Like many American journalists, I didn't know beans about Eastern Europe or how a communist party and government operated. Aware of how ignorant I was about history and politics, I was extremely careful when writing stories about the countries RFE broadcast to and asked many questions of others in the building who were from there or knew that part of the world. Special thanks go to Dino Drasal, whose many intellectual, musical and athletic gifts make him the most fascinating man I know. Dino was very patient and helpful in keeping me from embarrassing myself. If only he had shown those same qualities, the few times we were on a tennis court together.

Yes, the Central Intelligence Agency set RFE up and financed it originally, but I'm confident that during my ten years there none of my bosses in Central News worked for the CIA. (I was a TOM myself, an assistant news director for several years, and I certainly wasn't on the

CIA's payroll.) With one exception to be covered shortly, there were no efforts to slant stories nor hints that a certain item should be underplayed or ignored because it made our paymaster, the U.S. government, look bad. Central News provided the other desks thorough coverage of the Watergate mess. This is stated with confidence and conceit since this Yank wrote much of the Watergate material we put on the wire. (The day Richard Nixon resigned I was entertaining my parents who were visiting Munich. I loved Mom and Dad, but oh, was I dying to be at work that day.)

In 1976, during food riots in Poland, a top political analyst was in the newsroom a time or two looking at copy written by me and others. I had and have no problem with that. The analyst wanted to make sure we didn't say anything that would incite Poles to go out in the streets and cause trouble. RFE had been sharply criticized for appearing to encourage Hungarians to do that in the 1956 uprising before Soviet tanks were sent in to end it.

Speaking none of the languages in which RFE broadcast, I know little about the non-news programming, but people I trust say it was wide-ranging — economics, agriculture, religion, culture, sports, history and programs for young people. Six days a week the American managers in Munich issued a Recommended List of items from western newspapers that could or should be used in programming.

And there was good old western music. When an energetic Hungarian announcer-newscaster, Geza Ekecs, got his hands on new records from the West, he gave them titles in Hungarian, with the Central Newsroom sometimes helping him with the translation of the stranger ones. Once the records reached Radio Budapest they used the same titles, a strong indication someone there had been listening to RFE and Ekecs.

To my mind the only news story that RFE consistently botched was brief items on the U.S. Congress considering "alternate" means of financing Radio Free Europe and its sister station Radio Liberty, which broadcast to the Soviet Union. While our stories said Congress was debating whether to have the State Department pay RFE's and RL's bills, they failed to mention the bankroller at the time, the CIA. Every time a boss wrote one of these stories for the wire I argued that if we weren't going to own up to the arrangement with the CIA, we shouldn't do the story at all. The one item you shouldn't take shortcuts with was the one about your own organization. I was overruled every time.

(Newsrooms are notoriously bad in dealing with stories about themselves. When other news organizations learned from sources that CBS and General William Westmoreland, the former commander of U.S. troops in Vietnam, had agreed on a settlement of his libel suit against the network, CBS News executives, who knew the facts, wouldn't share them with the newsroom. CBS News, Radio broadcasts had to quote what newspapers and wire services were reporting about CBS. I was fortunate enough to be skiing in Austria at the time, or I might have said something I shouldn't have to the top TOMs.)

Some might argue that any dealings with the CIA taints you as a journalist. Baloney. On a home leave, I went to a party in Manhattan where a young man shook his head when he heard where I worked. I responded that I was willing to discuss the CIA and RFE if he could tell me the countries to which the station broadcast. Opinions are easy to come by. Facts are another matter. He couldn't meet my requirements so our chat was quite brief. I certainly wouldn't have defended the CIA's misdeeds in some areas, but its role at RFE, yes.

I will say that there was one guy in his late 20s or early 30s who roamed the halls at RFE, but no one seemed to know what he did. After the public disclosure that it was CIA money and not private donations from white-haired ladies in shawls that kept RFE in business, what this guy did was leave. Do I know why he left? No. Do I think I know? Yes. Do I care what he was? No. Because he had nothing at all to do with Central News.

In the summer of 2006, a quarter of a century after I left RFE, a PhD candidate writing a thesis about how newsrooms serving international audiences went about their business ran completely out of ideas and interviewed me. Out of my mouth came my usual assertion that RFE was the best place I ever worked. "Why?" she asked. After repeating what she already knew—that RFE frequently didn't report a major story unless it came from two news sources—I faltered and couldn't think of anything coherent to say. I knew it was true in my heart and in my bones, yet she was the first person to ever challenge me to provide specifics.

She got an email later that day.

It was the best newsroom I ever worked in because:

The rewrite desk was truly a rewrite desk. Many shops subscribe to more than one wire service, but the stories they use in print or on the air are frequently just the version of one service with perhaps a paragraph or two inserted from a second service, sometimes not too smoothly. The Intros (essentially wrap ups) written by the Central News Desk took everything we had on a story and usually turned out something much different from that of Reuters and UPI. The lead might have essentially been the same, but (the elements)… might have been stacked (the order in which they are presented) entirely different from anything we got from Reuters or UPI. At times our Intro might have emphasized an East European element Reuters or UPI paid little attention to.

Background and context were more important there than in any newsroom I ever worked in. You couldn't shorthand an American story, assuming your audience knew the background or mechanics, for example, of how the U.S. Congress or White House operates….

We were more careful about accuracy, more careful to delete unnecessary adjectives and more careful to avoid needless labeling of politicians and people than any other place I've worked.

It was not a shop afraid to correct stories or kill them. Journalists aren't good at admitting mistakes… There was a sense of urgency at Central News to correct what was wrong….

Everyone got read in time… My two most recent employers… have some shifts where people walk in…and start working, frequently without a clue of how the day's news has developed.

There were frequent conversations about writing…We old guys are amazed at how little talk there is in some shops about good writing. It doesn't seem to be part of the vocabulary of some people now working in journalism….

Although the PhD candidate thanked me for the email, I have no idea if my comments were of any value to her.

Another plus for Central News that I didn't mention was you didn't have to worry constantly that someone's political and social views would be reflected in his copy. At CBS News, a few anchors occasionally let their allegiances show in their story selection and wording. And unlike network radio, you weren't hindered at times in telling the news by a meaningless piece of tape an editor asked you to include.

Bavarian Apple-Throwing Champion

While Central News in Munich was a first-class news operation, I'm proud to report it still had its share of funsters and mavericks. An Australian lad decided to see if he could fly one night. He could, sort of. Keith — the name we'll give him — had enjoyed a liquid dinner in the RFE cafeteria, which offered an assortment of tasty adult beverages, and on returning to the newsroom urged his mates from the Commonwealth and the U.S. to "go down on your typewriters and really show McCoy how to write." Keith soon escalated his challenge by pouring a cup of coffee laced with brandy on my head. Although he was younger and bigger, I instinctively jumped from my chair and slugged him in the stomach. After he backed me up against the mailboxes, I told him I was going to get the guards. Heading toward the security office, I changed my mind. By the time I got back to the newsroom, Keith was gone. He had jumped out a window. Luckily for him, Central News was on the ground floor, and all he broke was an elbow.

Keith was a competent journalist when not drinking. It took a while, but two years or so later he got himself fired, basically because he drank too much. His leap to freedom that night was largely triggered by alcohol but probably also tinged by the tension that surfaced at times between the Americans in the newsroom and the chaps from the Commonwealth. We Yanks thought our brand of journalism was better, and we didn't think much of the habit of some of the Commonwealth types to, as they liked to say, "beat up" a story a little, meaning stretch the facts.

During my first stint at RFE, a senior desk editor, an Australian, insisted on hyphenating "to-day." It drove me nuts. He seemed so out of touch with the present that when editing stories about crop production in Eastern Europe I was surprised he didn't try to weave in a line from Chaucer about "the droughte of March hath perced to the roote."

By the time I returned to Munich for a second tour of duty, he had left or lyft as he might have put it.

I am glad to say the U.S. was fairly represented in the "gee, ain't he a character" department. We could claim credit for a genuine math whiz in Central News. You would go out for a drink with Marty, and when the check came he, who had four (4) Scotches to your two (2) beers, would always say, "Hey, Kid, let's split it." Marty wasn't a one dimensional person. He doubled as the main player in a game I call news pong. A gentleman we shall talk more about soon would hand Marty wire copy and say, "This is a good story. We should do something on it." After five minutes or so, Marty's name would be called again. "You know, Marty, that's a piece of shit. Let's forget it." Handing the copy back to the gentleman, Marty would offer, "Yeah, you're right. It's a piece of shit."

Ten minutes later—news pong isn't a fast game—the gentleman would serve again. "Sorry, Marty, I've changed my mind. I really think we ought to do that story. It's a damn good one." If Marty knew he was being had, he never let on. "You're right. It is a damn good story," he'd say and start looking at the copy one more time.

The inventor of news pong, yet another Australian, liked the ladies. He lived an apparent life of bliss because the ladies liked him too, and not the tubby ones but the foxes. If you saw him socially, he could be with X, with J, with N or even with his wife. One lunchtime as he was leaving the newsroom with an attractive woman I bellowed, "Good night." On his return from wherever it was he went to do whatever, he walked straight to my desk and simply said, "One of these days, McCoy, I'm going to kill you." I think he meant it.

Perhaps you're getting the impression that Aussie aces ruled the roost as far as lovable oddballs went. Indeed. And you have yet to meet exhibit A, the human humming machine. This son of Western Australia—home of the numbat, a squirrel-like animal with a long, sticky tongue—would sit at his desk humming at high pitch and volume while snipping a pair of scissors an inch from his lips. In between hums, he stuck out his tongue— much like I imagine a numbat would do— retracting it a millisecond before the scissors closed. It was hypnotic viewing to see if he would miss, a little like the guilty feeling you get at a carnival when staring at an extra large lady with three arms. You can't help yourself.

Prestidigitation, if that's what this was, is merely one of his talents. He—his real name is Roland Eggleston, although he would prefer to be addressed as "Your Lordship"—is a master at disappearing. You can be walking on a street with him conversing and between subject and verb he will vanish. Poof! One second he's shoulder-to-shoulder with you. The next he's nowhere to be seen. It is hard to keep his attention even when you think you are being terribly entertaining. He will spot something in a shop or down a side street, and, while you labor on in your explanation of the world's six major truths, he has slipped away to see the sights. It is this curiosity and eagerness to explore dark alleys that make him a top-notch reporter, something the TOMs finally let him do after acknowledging that his work on the desk was basically a lot of humming and scissoring.

His Lordship has reported from many East-West conferences, and diplomats of all persuasions know him and his dedication to getting as close to the truth as he can. He tells marvelous stories about private discussions on nights out with the diplomatic corps.

If you can't tell it by now, Roley is one of my best friends. We have spent many a day skiing and many a night boozing and talking. He's always saying or doing something interesting or funny or at least a wee bit askew. I love him.

When my mother first heard that I had accepted a job at Radio Free Europe, she asked, "Is there any danger?" "Nah," I said. That's before I met Kyle, the champion apple thrower of Bavaria, indoor division. One of the perks at RFE for most non-Germans in Central News was free housing. Kyle was always in a stew about his house or the appliances and furniture. He was in frequent telephone contact with the housing department, and if the conversation went badly Kyle would swear, stand up and throw, as hard as he could, a half-eaten apple against the wall. He reacted the same way, but not as often, when a story he had spent considerable time on fell apart because of new developments or other reasons.

A good journalist whose real name is Colin Duck also worked at RFE for a while. Although I don't know if he was ever on duty when Kyle did his apple-against-the-wall trick, I would have loved to have heard someone shout, "Duck, Duck."

I'll bet Colin, an Australian, is about as tired of duck jokes as I am of people asking, "Are you the real McCoy?" That said, months before Duck arrived, management issued a note about his hiring. On dull nights in the newsroom you could hear people—okay, you could hear me—sitting around and going "quack, quack."

Your tax dollars at work.

13

Bosses: Dumb. Duh-Dumb. Dumb.

When a young person sits down with an old person for a beer, the one with smooth skin frequently asks, "How in the world did Adam Sandler get into management?" There is no answer to this question. The world is simply full of mysteries that must be accepted. Not to accept them is bad for you, leads to craziness and contributes to global warming.

During my senior year at Indiana University, I was a paid announcer-disc jockey at WFIU, the school's FM radio station run by a genius who never appeared in public without a wet cigar in his mouth. He directed the DJs to keep a close eye on the VU meter in the broadcast console to make sure it never, ever dropped below a certain minimum level. His reasoning (how's that for misusing the English language?) was that if the station piped all its classical music out at the same volume those on the fringes of our listening area would be able to hear us better. Crescendos? The hell with crescendos. Following orders, we cranked up Ravel's "Bolero" to get rid of all that repetitious, soft crap. If Monsieur Ravel ever felt like banging his head against his coffin, this would have been the time.

The boss at UPI's National Radio wire banned the words "harass" and "harassment" in our copy. Those were bad radio words, he said, because too many announcers stressed the "ass" part. Based on such logic, he could have also—but thank God didn't—blacklisted "sock" because it sounded like "cock," "duck" because it rhymed with a popular expletive, and, if there were a big story in Saskatchewan, we could only hope it didn't happen in Regina.

During the Vietnam War, the chief of ABC Radio News would walk into the New York newsroom as briefings by officials and reports from correspondents in Saigon were fed in on a noisy circuit. My memory says whenever there was a particularly loud hiss on the line, making it nearly impossible to make out more than every third or fourth word, the head man would declare, "Hey, Guys, Saigon sure sounds good this morning." Boy, it sure does. Or, in the Saigon-speak of the day, "oy-su-do." Because of that nudge from the top, all morning long the ABC Radio crew slapped tape on the air from Saigon that listeners, especially those in cars, could barely understand a word of. It looked good though on the copy editor's log when an entry said you had used natural sound and an on-scene report from a correspondent in South Vietnam. To be fair I felt this was the man's only blind spot as leader of a news operation, but a big one. Otherwise, he was aces.

While a TOM, I was the assistant for a while to a professional phone operator. My superior was always on the phone, almost always on personal business. Calls were made to the spouse, the spouse returned the calls. On and on it went, none of it having anything to do with the news business. There were many other personal calls that dragged on endlessly. Should there be a lull in the ring-a-ling, my boss would—what else?—go to lunch. Here was someone way ahead of the curve. This was long before cell phones and smartphones, long before nearly every pissant and his cousin were permanently staring at and fiddling with one of those devices on the street, in the car, at the gym, in the bathroom, in bed.

The worst time of my professional life came in 1987 during a long writers' strike at CBS News. I and other TOMs from the news division were working twelve hours a day, seven days a week, surrounded by executives, sales people, secretaries and other non-union non-journalists from the Radio Division who were told to do phone interviews and to pick the newsiest parts for newscasts. While well-intentioned, they were very slow and not accustomed to my brusqueness. When it appeared the strike was about to end, a vice president of the Radio Division confided that he had been offered $100 to punch me out. I said that didn't sound like a lot of money. "It isn't," he said, "but think of the satisfaction."

To keep the two radio networks operating around the clock, managers from several bureaus were brought to New York to run the copy desks. The TOM of TOMs at CBS, Laurence Tisch, a man of many great ideas, decided a writers' strike would be the perfect time to toss some managers out on the street too. Among those fired was Tom Newberry, assistant bureau manager in Atlanta, who had worked his ass off for radio without a murmur about missing his bed and his family or existing on food from the CBS cafeteria. An hour or so after he got the word, the scheduler in radio, unaware of what had happened, asked him to stay later than usual that day. Knowing we were in trouble, he said "yes."

I lost it. CBS News didn't deserve Tom Newberry or me. I found myself at the back of the newsroom crying. Not with tears in my eyes, crying, damn close to sobbing. I was exhausted and angry and felt badly misused. Every morning and evening I saw the faces of the writers on the picket line, good people trying to make a living. With no money coming in, a couple of them were driving limousines to pay their bills. My crying in the newsroom proved to be a learning moment. I finally realized why you work hard and try to excel. You don't do it for a company or a cause or a paycheck. You do it for yourself. You are proud of what you do and want to do your best all the time. If you mess up or fall short, there is no one more disappointed than yourself. It had taken me about a quarter of a century to discover this. Tom Newberry did fine after leaving CBS. Good for you, Tom.

(Bonuses were given to managers after the strike. I gave part of mine to the Writers Guild. Lufthansa Airlines got another big chunk. The day after a settlement was announced I boarded a plane to go skiing in Austria.)

Before you get the idea that a fondness for bad timing was limited to bosses in Manhattan, let me introduce you to a TOM in the Central Newsroom at Radio Free Europe when I was an editor there. On the day West Germany was scheduled to sign a key agreement with Poland, a boss came rushing up to my desk.

"German TV says they aren't going to sign the agreement. You'd better put something out," meaning write a story for the English language news wire that the Polish and other nationality services could translate for their newscasts.

I asked, "What do you mean 'they aren't going to sign the agreement' ? They aren't going to sign it today? Or they're never going to sign it?"

"I don't know. All German TV said was: 'They aren't going to sign the agreement.' You'd better put something out," the TOM repeated.

Whipping out my own repeater, I screamed, "What the fuck is it I'm supposed to write? They're not going to sign the agreement ever or they're just not going to sign it until later today?"

"I don't know. That's all they said," he said once more.

At some point the TOM declared, "You're going to die of a heart attack." To which I responded, "Maybe, but I'm not going to die from taking bullshit off managers." That was more or less my unwavering motto until the day I left the business.

I eventually wrote a vague item, saying there was a report by a German television network that the signing had been delayed. Period. Full stop. RFE had a German Desk to handle German stories and to monitor German media. The person supposed to be watching things on this eventful day had gone to lunch. And whose fault was that? The TOMs, of course. (I later became a TOM at RFE, my first fling as one. Let's face it, when you're offered more money it's hard to refuse.)

Most newsrooms keep upgrading the technology their editors and writers use. Most newsrooms. A big cheese at one employer ordered SpellCheck removed from the computers because it was letting too many misspelled words get through. Horse feathers. We working class stiffs heard another, more believable story. This manager had written a piece containing several references to a politician, all of which were mangled by SpellCheck. They all came out as "Spitfire." No one in the newsroom apparently noticed this until Mr. "Spitfire" called and identified himself as Spitzer. Eliot Spitzer, New York Attorney General.

Everyone needs an editor, right? Right. Whoever handled the copy didn't catch that every "Spitzer" in the copy had been corrupted to "Spitfire." To me the sensible solution would have been to call the luckless person in, reduce him or her to tears in the privacy of a small office, followed by a strong reminder that the copy of TOMs, even the holiest among them, should be handled no differently than anyone else's. It must be carefully checked. Computer tools shouldn't be blindly depended on for accuracy. That didn't happen. SpellCheck was shot down by "Spitfire."

"We Can't Have the Desk Second-guessing Reporters All the Time."

Every news organization I've known had one thing in common: the Washington bureau, from the manager on down, was convinced that the folks at headquarters were full of shit and had no news judgment. Naturally, headquarters felt the same way about the DC bureau.

Living in Washington for a long time can warp your power of reasoning, making you think that all of America is consumed every hour of every day with politics (who's hot and who's not) and leaving you terrified that the slightest misstep will cost you access to the politicians and string pullers at the top. This dangerous distortion of reality can seduce TOMs into trying to interfere with the news.

In January of 1984, when nearly everyone except maybe the pandas at the National Zoo knew President Ronald Reagan was going to run for a second term, the Republicans bought time on CBS-TV for "the Gipper" to formally announce his intentions. Minutes before the words about running again came out of Reagan's mouth, a copy of *The New York Times* arrived in the radio newsroom, citing sources as saying he would. I remember a call from the radio desk and responding that if we could find out that copies of *The Times* were available to the general public and not just the CBS newsroom then the story was fair game. The radio desk called *The New York Times*. Yes, the paper was on the street, so CBS Radio broke the "news" before Reagan did.

The TOMs at CBS News pooped their pants. Radio newsroom phones rang, my home phone rang again. Serious money had been paid to CBS Television so Reagan could reveal this "news" on his own. By reporting the decision ahead of time, Radio had sinned and sinned badly. The Washington bureau chief demanded that everyone involved in this breach send him a note about what happened and why radio did what it did. What did it did? It reported the news.

The following day much of my time was spent rehashing for TOMs radio's actions and the reasons behind it. Late in the day John Lane, a fine man as well as a vice president, came to my office, asked what kind of day I had, and then patted me on the back, a welcome gesture that I interpreted as John saying, "I know what we've put you and the radio desk through is bullshit and not journalism." (In revisiting this, I found that at least one person on duty that night didn't think I was as supportive of his actions as I should have been. If I wasn't, sorry.)

The tension and distrust between headquarters and the Wonderful Washington Bureau (WWB) can be exacerbated in shops where reporters have more clout than editors. A correspondent from one WWB once covered a speech by a government official and missed what little news was in it, or at least that's what I thought. Having a transcript of the remarks, this bashful lad from Clinton County, Indiana, wrote his own version of what was said.

What happened next, you ask? Yes, the correspondent called all upset, and, yes, then the bureau manager called all upset. I was told by the fiery WWB boss that "we can't have the desk second-guessing reporters all the time." Huh? I responded forcefully and logically, "That's what desk people do." My recollection is that after reading my take on the speech the bureau manager allowed as how it was a better, newsier story than the one the correspondent filed.

Another day I objected to a piece of copy from the WWB that referred to an upcoming meeting of world leaders as a gathering of "heads of state." When I pointed out to the bureau chief that some of the leaders were "heads of government," I was told the "terms are interchangeable." Right. So there isn't a tuppence worth of difference between the Queen of England and the British prime minister. Rubbish.

On one occasion, a bureau manager wrote a story himself about changes in the military command in Iraq. I gave it to the newest member of the staff, telling him to re-write it and make the third paragraph the lead. The re-write led with the announcement that the general now in charge planned to go see the troops in Iraq. The original lead from WWB focused on a bunch of meetings the general had with a bunch of nobodies. The bureau manager-author wasn't consulted about this change, and I understand went a little crazy on the phone with one or more of the other 768 TOMs. Several of those managers, by the way, privately agreed the surgery we did to the story made it stronger.

Because of the schism between headquarters and Washington, it was perfectly logical for one WWB manager to issue a lavish note of praise after his reporters had missed damn near every major story coming out of a national political convention. "They didn't run with the pack," the note crowed.

Yep. They sure didn't. They attended an entirely different convention than other reporters. They uncovered minutiae while others spotted news. No one else had the "stories" they wrote because they weren't worth having. Quite an accomplishment. Notes like those were always disappointing to a staff trained to spot garbage and hyperbole and were quickly recirculated with scurrilous, but totally appropriate, comments.

This brings us to one fine summer day when I was reading in and noticed a BULLETIN from WWB about police being summoned to a meeting of the House Ways and Means Committee. Not long afterward, a committee member, Democrat Lloyd Doggett, appeared on CNN to say he was "outraged." My little corner of the newsroom did a story on this. CNN then aired video from angry members on the House floor condemning the unseemly remarks made at the closed committee meeting. CNN soon had a verbatim of the objectionable comments, which included Congressman Pete Stark calling Congressman Scott McInnis a "fruitcake." (I know it's hard to imagine a member of one party saying that about a member of another.)

In a few minutes, the WWB sent a new story, and the reporter who wrote it was on the phone to answer a question or two from an editor near me. Always the nosy one, I asked the editor, "Does she know about the fruitcake quote?" After a pause, the editor nodded, and it was agreed that we would insert "fruitcake" elements from our end.

We had moved on to other tasks when up to the desk came one of the many, many TOMs. "What's this about fruitcake?" he asked. As I understand it, the WWB manager sent an email to the Supremo Bosso of my unit, and although he had left for the day he called the newsroom to speak to another TOM to find out what this fruitcake business was all about. This is having your eyes on the big picture, yes? Otherwise they wouldn't be trading important messages on the subject of fruitcakes.

The quote was in our story as it should have been. The denizens of the WWB didn't always warmly welcome suggestions from headquarters where surly serfs periodically tampered with the precious copy of reporters and engaged in that unspeakable practice of second-guessing them. Whoever heard of such a thing?

14

What Does It Mean When You Dream About Burying a Chicken?

It sure is easy to make fun of other people and their mistakes, stupidities, and shortcomings. Knock on wood, I've never done anything half as dumb as some of the bozos already mentioned or about to be.

Well, there was the time at UPI when a BULLETIN on the main newspaper wire said the train carrying President Kennedy home from the Army-Navy football game had left the siding in Philadelphia. I quickly pounded out a BULLETIN for the radio wire. Several minutes passed with nothing more on the A wire about a terrifying accident. As I began to fret about this unexplainable lapse, a wiser person pointed out the original BULLETIN was simply notifying subscribers that the president's train was heading back to Washington. Oh!

I suppose I could also confess that throughout the days following Kennedy's assassination, I kept putting copy on the radio wire, stating that the late president was going to be "buried at Arlington National CEREMONY." Hey, both the word I wanted, "cemetery," and the word I wrote begin with a "c" and end with a "y."

This was the beginning of my realization that I was a poor editor of my own copy. I saw words that weren't there. What the hell, now that I've started....

The day China's Mao Tse-tung died I wrote a fast and fairly long story for Radio Free Europe's English-language wire about who he was and what he had done, a good deal of it off the top of my head. I was quite pleased with it, and, best of all, my boss liked it too and sent me a note about what a fine piece of journalism it was. Then the evening shift came in, and a whiz kid discovered a mistake—in the #$%^ first sentence. I believe it had to do with how long Mao had been party leader. Damn! After all these years, it still bothers me. Attention: Bob Millington. I always liked you until you opened your mouth that day.

As a writer at CBS News, I frequently ran into trouble when assigned to do think pieces, something other than a quick and dirty, uncomplicated news story. I couldn't get rolling until I wrote a lead I liked, never accepting that you may never come up with the perfect opening sentence to a commentary, but you must get something down on paper or in the computer and hope you have time to go back and improve it. Roger Mudd, sitting in one day on Walter Cronkite's radio commentary, wanted to kill me after I handed him a script at the last second that was not only incoherent and loaded with crossed out words, it had the added disadvantage of being thirty seconds short. As far as I know, Mudd doesn't have Charlie Osgood's musical talents, or otherwise he could have hummed and strummed a banjo to eat up that long gap. I don't remember what we did to fill the time (probably ran an extra commercial), but I haven't forgotten the Mudd glare. I didn't get many of these assignments and for that CBS Radio's listeners, affiliates and anchors should be grateful.

As noted earlier, during my days in management the news staff at CBS News, Radio won two cherished Peabody Awards, one for the crisis in China that culminated in the protests and slaughter in Tiananmen Square and the other for coverage of the assassination of Israeli Prime Minister Yitzhak Rabin. Although I'm proud of that, there were many times when I was a horrible manager, especially in sending reporters quickly to a breaking story. Maybe I dawdled because I've always detested a staple of modern broadcasting—the frequent and repetitious LIVE reports from the scene that contain absolutely no new information. (For several days after the bombing at the Boston Marathon in 2013, CNN had reporters standing in the street interviewing each other (yes, I said, interviewing each other) with little or nothing new to say, and some of the things said were dead wrong.)

Two instances in which I inexplicably didn't make a move to get someone to the scene—a plane crash on the East Coast that killed about fifteen people and a shooting at an Arkansas school—led to either a boss at CBS News or a fellow journalist questioning where my head was and why we had no reporter on site.

It Was the Olympics, You Moron!

My biggest screwup of all, at least the one I know about, was my failure to order immediate wall-to-wall coverage on CBS Radio after a bomb went off at the Olympics in Atlanta. Somehow it didn't seem all that big a deal to me. It was late at night. There didn't appear to be that many serious casualties or that much damage. In reviewing this blunder thousands of times, I recall my biggest concern that night was not wanting to miss a scheduled therapy session for an ailing right knee the next morning. Ski season wasn't that far off, and I wanted to get the knee ready.

I still shake my head when I think about it. We did at least one special every hour on the bombing, and the story dominated our newscasts. But no wall-to-wall coverage. Dumb. Very, very dumb. It was the OLYMPICS, you moron!

I was lucky enough to be on vacation when Princess Diana was killed. I have always had a blind spot about anything to do—and I do mean anything—with the British royal family. If I hadn't been loafing in Maine, I'm fairly sure I would have told the desk to do very little except report the story on regular newscasts. The way I saw it she was a slut who divorced a twit to run off with a junkie. A top television news producer, who wasn't on vacation but perhaps shared some of my sentiments, didn't go wild over the story and lost his job. CBS Radio was saved by Charlie Kaye, an excellent newsman, who instantly realized that lots of folks would care a great deal about the death of Princess Di and ordered continuing live coverage of the accident in Paris and reaction to it.

One last admission and that's it. All too often when I was a TOM, I was terrible at handling people. If I had a problem with how a story was told, spotted a factual error or thought a key element was left out, my natural reaction was sarcasm and ridicule rather than a more constructive approach of making my views known and suggesting they be considered the next time around. This wasn't very productive in the long run with many people.

Now let me use these last two paragraphs to try to rekindle sympathy. I have a recurring bad dream about the news business. It's been the same for years. I'm writing a newscast for a well-known anchor, and I can't find enough meaty stories to fill it. There is nothing but inconsequential items to pick from, and every time I find something I think worth doing I change my mind. I then get flustered. Not good in any profession.

In one of the most recent versions, I dreamt I was outside a house with Barry Griffiths, a friend and fellow manager from RFE, helping him bury a chicken. Did the chicken represent bad stories the two of us had done over the years that we wanted to get rid of for good? Or was it a symbol of our faulty management styles that we were hoping to hide? Any psychiatrists willing to take a crack at analyzing what this means are urged to visit my website at deadchickens.edu. Please hurry.

15

"Oh, so We Were a Little Off."

*W*hile journalists are among the first to object when politicians or companies try to cover up something bad or questionable, many of us are world-class cowards when we mess up, downplaying the significance of a mistake, perhaps even arguing what we wrote wasn't really that far off, that wrong.

A CBS News White House correspondent filed a report late one afternoon that Hamilton Jordan, the ex-Carter White House Chief of Staff, had an "inoperable" form of cancer. You always go with your guy, right? Right.

The phones began to ring shortly afterward, and I found myself talking to Jody Powell, a newspaper columnist who had been President Jimmy Carter's press secretary. Powell was livid. The story was wrong. There was no basis to it. "I told Lesley not to go with it," Powell screamed, referring to chief White House correspondent Lesley Stahl. I don't know if the reporter who filed the Jordan story had talked to Stahl before he called us. (Reconstructing this, I don't believe we ever reported what kind of cancer Jordan had, but around this time, 1985, he was diagnosed with lymphoma.)

Powell said in effect that CBS News was such a shit house that he was going to do a column on us. I had never met Powell nor ever talked to him before, but I suggested a column about an honest error CBS News had made wouldn't be very interesting to readers. I kept stressing if we had it wrong we wanted to get it right and correct ourselves on the air. After at least two phone calls from Powell, I was comfortable with what we knew. Jordan did have cancer, but it wasn't inoperable. I started writing a correction for the next broadcast.

In between the Powell phone calls, there had been others from two CBS News vice presidents. One of the VPs was a buddy of Dan Rather who specialized in pointing out the obvious, let us say marching over to the radio desk to announce, "We're not using that story in the Italian papers about Bush grabbing Mrs. Gorbachev's ass" or some equally preposterous crap that no one with an ounce of sense would think of using. (At least back then. Now if there were such a story, it might be a lead.) He wasn't the only vice president of news to say asinine things. He merely said them more often than the others.

The other VP on the phone was the Washington bureau chief, and the way you keep that job in many big organizations is to devote every ounce of energy to creating turf and then protecting it at all costs. When I told him what Powell had said — that Hamilton Jordan had cancer but it wasn't "inoperable" — he replied, "Oh, so we were a little off." I suppose I wanted him to shout "oh fuck!" or "shit!" or "God damn it! How did we screw that up?" — something a little higher up the scale of indignation. Nope. All I got was, "Oh, so we were a little off."

While Irene and friends were waiting for me at a Manhattan restaurant, I was stuck in my office, working on a correction. It took me a while, as usual, to catch on. Why was the lowly executive editor of radio news, me, scripting a correction and then running it by two vice presidents? Turf, good old turf. With the peons of radio in New York handling the correction, it kept the stain off the Washington bureau as well as the CBS Evening News with Dan Rather.

Being First and Wrong and Proud of It

Being a little off can also mean not right in the head, out of touch with reality. That happens in newsrooms sometimes. Reporters, desk people, managers think they may be on to a big story, get in a hurry, want it to be true and become careless. It can be contagious. No one steps back, takes charge and demands, "Let's all calm down."

An editor took a call one night from a reporter about the Chinese yuan. For years the U.S. government had berated Beijing for keeping tight controls on the exchange rate of the yuan against the dollar, but now there were headlines and bells because a Chinese official said China thought its currency should be flexible, precisely what Washington had been urging. A hell of a story, if true. Aye, there's the rub.

The official—a man we will call Yuan Spin—was initially identified as a member of a Chinese banking committee then later as an advisor to the body. Huh? Shouldn't that have triggered a question or two? Was he speaking in an official capacity or merely showing off late at night in a foreign country where it was hard to concentrate with all those painted, tanned and perhaps available women everywhere you looked? Shouldn't that small but essential detail be in the story? Not the part about the painted women, but the business about whether he was speaking for his country or simply engaging in late night BS?

There's nothing wrong—in fact, it's a damn good idea when a story first breaks—to acknowledge that "it wasn't immediately clear" what impact THIS would have on THAT. If, and this is an outlandish example, reporters learned that the secretary of homeland security, a man who had been under fire for questionable aspects of his personal life, was seen naked in the office of the Russian ambassador to the U.S., a smart desk person would insist that fairly early on a sentence be inserted in the copy, saying "it wasn't immediately clear what the two men were doing together or if the incident would have any impact on their jobs."

No lights went off in anyone's head when the first take on the remarks of the Chinese official said he belonged to the important banking committee, but the second take described him as merely an adviser. Judging by how things were going, the official's rank might soon be whittled down to that of the banking committee's chauffeur.

Although in our scenario the importance of the Chinese official was never cleared up that evening, the following day the TOMs were very pleased. Pleased because, although the reporter and the desk didn't quite know who this character was, they were the first to report his comments. And that means kudos all around. Kudos from the TOMs. Nothing better than that.

The note of congratulations not only raved that the newsroom beat all the competition with the official's musings, it gleefully noted how long it took the other services to match the story. The note went on to say the newsroom made all the TOMs doubly proud by being ahead of the competition when the Chinese government denied the story, when Beijing said Yuan Spin was speaking only for himself and not his country.

Wouldn't you think there might have been at least one TOM who spoke up and asked the other suits what was so bloody wonderful about being first with a story that was poorly sourced and wrong and then being first again when there was high-level confirmation of its wrongness? This sounds so amateurish that it couldn't possibly have happened, right? Don't bet on it.

16

A Few Kind Words, Finally, for Guys With Razor Blades

"Just" is a terrible word to use when talking about what someone does for a living.

"You mean she's just a hairdresser?"

"He's just a bartender at Outback."

How demeaning. They're both honorable professions, even if I have strong views about which of the two civilized society could really do without.

A man in his 50s, who had spent most of his life working at CBS Radio, introduced himself to the president of CBS News by saying, "I'm just a tech." Just a tech? Hello, Mr. Technician. When I was working on West 57th Street, there would have been no CBS News On The Hour if you and your buddies didn't see that the right switches were thrown when they should be so the broadcast got on and off the air on time and that the right tapes were played in the order the anchor expected. Sounds pretty important to me, and it should to you too.

Perhaps he slipped in the "just" to needle the CBS News chief about the diminishing importance the company places on the value of radio techs in every new contract with their union, the IBEW. When I started at ABC Radio in the '60s, it was a union violation for a writer, a member of the Writers Guild of America, to touch the start or stop buttons on a tape machine, let alone pick up a razor blade and cut a piece of tape. By 1998, when I left broadcasting, writers were doing almost everything that formerly was the sole province of technicians, including making sound bites.

The techs still employed in network radio handle maintenance on equipment and studios or are assigned to Master Control where they make sure commercials and programs play on time to the proper parts (or "legs") of the network. Master Control is far more complex than I am capable of explaining, and at CBS Radio the IBEW has lost exclusive jurisdiction even in that vital nerve center and must share space and duties with non-union people. Anchors and writer-producers are now in charge of turning on microphones, playing the sound bites and overseeing any live elements (interviews with newsmakers or correspondents) in the broadcast.

If I had a quarter for every time a tech at CBS or ABC saved a broadcast I was involved in, I would own three houses instead of one. Why is the smart aleck who many pages ago made fun of the tech on the overnight with "soiled jeans, dirty white socks and a filthy sweater" now all gaga with praise? I'll tell you why. Merely because someone is odd as all get-out doesn't mean he doesn't know how to do his job and do it well. (Managers: remember this the next time a disheveled, lard-face guy, wearing an "If Only I Were A Woman" T-shirt gets real close to you and asks if you have any work he can do.)

With fewer techs around, I can't imagine that working in network radio is nearly as enjoyable as it once was. What a shame. I was amused, entertained and enlightened by many a tech and am glad I was.

A good tech could handle any curve ball thrown his way. Last second surprises—additions or subtractions from the original line up of tapes and live shots for the broadcast—didn't bother or fluster him. He was cool amid chaos and noise. If disaster seemed about to happen, he usually kicked it out of the way and joked later about how close we had come. (If you're wondering why there are all these male pronouns, most of the techs I knew—good, bad and indifferent—were men.)

A top-notch tech was a magician at cutting tape quickly, getting everything ready for last second phone calls from correspondents and politicians, putting a scratchy phone line from Beirut through a noise filter to make it easier to understand, and handling fifteen other things. But perhaps his most crucial skill was figuring out, most of the time, what a writer-producer meant to say when giving instructions right before air time. Many times the frantically mumbled last-second words from the writer-producer weren't very clear at all.

I want to pay tribute to a few wizards, real characters who have been given made-up names. As you read on, maybe you'll see why I decided to do that.

Roger Parker. A delight to work with, Roger loved the horses and the ladies — perhaps in the opposite order, although it was sometimes hard to tell — and was adept at making late cuts of tape, including editing a fresh sound bite after a broadcast had started and having it ready to play when the anchor called for it. He could be absolutely spectacular. Roger was from the Caribbean and when he got excited he spoke extremely fast, making him, at least to my ear, hard to understand.

"Speak English, Roger," I would yell at him. His response was always to shout back, "I am speaking English" and then to take his large right hand and grab his crotch. This was years before Michael Jackson was doing it on videos. Jackson was an amateur compared to Roger.

Captain Radio. Another giant. I called him Captain Radio because he always had a headset on, listening to tapes of old rock groups. Consequently he always talked louder than he needed to. Bobbing his head to the music he was hearing never seemed to interfere with whatever he needed to do for CBS and doing it very well and fast. Anyone who doesn't believe that beings from other planets are among us has never seen Captain Radio in action.

Bart Wheeler. A true craftsman who you wanted to be on hand when a major singer or musician died. He was the best there was at mixing and incorporating music into a script to create a stirring portrait of sound. His vice was pictures, vacation pictures. If you ran into him after he had a week off, he'd say, "I wanna show you some pictures of the Galapagos. We were there last week." He would then start handing you, one by one, pictures from what looked like a stack of four thousand. You prayed that a story would come along that would keep both of you busy as hell for the next three or four hours so there would be little time for pictures.

The most interesting aspect of looking at Bart's vacation shots was to see if the "we" he was talking about this time involved the same lady who appeared in the last "we" batch. Some "we" members disappeared, only to return a year or so later. Although I never did, I should have asked how you got back on the "we" team after once being sidelined.

On a frantic day when there were two or three big stories and you were lucky to be working with a talented tech, you hoped he wasn't about to go home. "How long are you here?" I would ask on such days. The favorite answer of many techs was "Till I'm sixty-five."

In my TOM days, I always tried to remember to thank the technicians after instant specials, complicated newscasts or after a long, hard day of blockbuster news. I probably didn't thank them nearly enough, so listen up, Techs: thank you, thank you, thank you. (At ABC I think we called them engineers. The guys at CBS didn't like to be called that. "We don't drive trains," they'd say.)

It was my pleasure to have worked at ABC with, among others, Dick Aronson, Gene Carlson, Neil Pultz, Eddie Salzman, and Jerry Sheen and at CBS with, among others, Matt DeLieto, Mort Goldberg, Steve Gregoli, Roger Hirsch, Steve Kirsch, Henry Lenz, Keith Parke, Dave Saviet, Gary Scherer, Ed Sentner, Tom Sheehy, Art Starr, Leslie Tatz, Andy Vallon and Phil Yanatelli.

There were also technicians who did a decent job but were annoying, primarily because they never could comprehend why editorial priorities might change, that an editor and anchor might decide at the last moment to rearrange the order of the entire newscast because of a new development or reevaluation of the impact of a certain story. Some techs saw that as nothing more than a bad case of indecision by the editorial side. "The desk can't make up its mind" was their sentiment.

Others in the business a long time, surprisingly, didn't appreciate how sound from the scene of a story — flood waters, sirens, heavy winds or pounding hammers — could add atmosphere and understanding to a radio report. One tech resisted mixing the sound of pealing bells into a report by a correspondent in Rome.

"We're not children," the technician said. "If the reporter says the bells rang, we believe him. They rang. We don't have to fucking hear them." It was incredible when it happened twenty-five years ago and remains so today.

And there were the others. Guys with twelve thumbs who specialized in somehow leaving a bleep or extraneous noise at the end of most sound bites they made. Theirs was a rare talent. They swore the cut was fine the way it was. Ask them to do anything the least bit tricky or last moment and a train wreck was virtually guaranteed. Enough. Let's not dwell on these fellows. They at least knew Bangkok wasn't the capital of all Southeast Asia, unlike that lad pretending to be a journalist.

Thanks are also long overdue to teletype operators at RFE's central newsroom and at UPI's National Radio wire. Most of the RFE operators were German women who spoke English well enough to spot a typo or an incorrect word in the English copy they were given. At UPI one remarkable human being, earning a living as a teletype operator, frequently caught wrong sports scores and suggested I double check them. Barney was also the only operator I ever met who loved to take a piece of copy, turn it upside down and then type away at full speed. All the words came out flawlessly on the radio wire. It was wonderful to watch.

In those pre-politically correct times, Barney was the source of many uplifting epigrams I had never heard before or since. For example, "You know what a surprise is? A fart with a lump in it." While this may be an unpopular view, I believe newsrooms were better places to work and turned out a better product when you didn't have to watch your God damn language every fucking second and if you wanted to smoke, you did. Piss on decorum.

Long live Barney's spirit!

17

A Life Spent in What Is Now, All Too Often, a Frivolous Profession

I was over sixty years old when I first heard it, damn near eligible for Social Security after four decades of dealing with Sputnik, assassinations in Dallas and Memphis, rioting in America's streets, Vietnam, a man on the moon, the lies of Richard Nixon, an awful Sunday morning in Beirut that left more than two hundred U.S. Marines dead, the Gulf War, the collapse of the sham called the Soviet Union, and on and on.

It was only three words long. A good radio sentence. "It's show business," the man said. There it was, right out in the open and here all this time I thought I was in the news business. I swear I started out in news and had gone about my work almost religiously. Then a woman cut off a man's penis and it got picked up (both the penis and the story), Tonya Harding had some friends take care of a competitor, O.J. took himself and all of us for a ride, and the world I had always known got turned upside down.

I was as guilty as anyone. These were legitimate news stories, no? I sure thought so at the time. Maybe it was the ceaseless day after day, hour after hour emphasis on them that led to a redefining of what was considered worthy of inclusion in a newscast. "It's show business," the man said, walking through the CBS News, Radio newsroom where he was now in charge and his credo was all that mattered.

When you're in show business, you won't be around long if you're BORING. Ya gotta keep things moving. Gotta keep the stories zippy, sassy and breezy (ZSB). So say *auf Wiedersehen* to most foreign stories. They are so lacking in ZSB. Even stories from countries where thousands of American troops are stationed. Dump'em. What ya want to zero in on is the sorry road apples that much of television and radio jump up and down on with such enthusiasm and fervor: anything involving sex, celebrities and unrepentant trash of all kinds — white, black, Asian, butterscotch, whatever. That's the real news, or what passes for it, much of the time now on many radio and TV outlets and websites.

And surveys and studies. Oh my God! Sorry. OMG! Ya gotta love surveys and studies. No need to tell listeners who bankrolls them or how reliable past surveys have proved to be. Just throw them on the air.

"CBS News. I'm Seldom Hardly. Oh, oh. Better skip those double cheeseburgers at lunch today. A survey just out by the Food Safety Network finds that if you eat two double cheeseburgers every day for 16 weeks you'll end up with…big buns of your own."

What a shocker. And what the hell is the Food Safety Network? Who runs it and how does it get its financing? Who knows? Who cares? It's show business. No time to explain all that. Gotta keep things moving, gotta keep it ZSB.

> Memo To Jesus Christ:
> "Dear Sir,
> "If you're thinking about coming back any time soon, better make sure it's not the same day as some smartly-named outfit releases a survey about Americans' driving habits or a study comes out on the ten best cities in which to own a dog. You won't have a chance of getting much time on morning radio or television against such heavyweight competition.
> "Respectfully yours,
> "Larry McCoy
> "P.S. I was baptized in three different churches, two Protestant, one Catholic. Is that going to pay off somewhere down the road?"

How did we get here? The old line "everyone's a comedian" pops into mind. Program directors at stations where news had always been taken seriously saw that Howard Stern and others blabbing all morning long about body parts — their own and others — had good numbers as did Don Imus who mocked and interviewed top politicians and journalists about major issues of the day. Why not try to grab part of that demographic by spicing up what stations presented as news and have it encompass starlets and harlots as well as lots and lots of "news you can use," warm and fuzzy bits about health, food, and saving money that had traditionally been relegated to the back of the newspaper or the tail end of a newscast, if included at all?

That's mostly speculation on my part because I had little chance to listen to either Stern or Imus. When they were on, I was either reading the paper on the train headed for the office or already there with other things to worry about. All I know is that TV and radio news got so messed up that what used to be considered kickers — the activities, legal or otherwise, of stars and celebrities or the odd but relatively unimportant human interest items written to close newscasts — are now considered major "stories," worthy at times of being the lead.

With show business as their mandate, editors and anchors at CBS Radio began looking to Hollywood for their inspiration. On two mornings in 1999 the most important story of the day for CBS Radio was the opening of widely-hyped movies. The Tom Cruise, Nicole Kidman movie "Eyes Wide Shut" led two newscasts one morning. Yes, the lead, the first item. Another time the assistant to Mr. Show Business called the producer of "The CBS World News Roundup" shortly before air time to make sure he understood that the lead that morning had to be the latest Star Wars movie, "The Phantom Menace."

Is not something really out of whack when "The CBS World News Roundup," a distinguished broadcast going all the way back to 1938, starts the day sounding like "Entertainment Tonight"? I had lived long enough to see a serious profession, mine, become a frivolous one. A joke.

Making fun of what's on the news, how it's presented and those presenting it has become a separate industry. The packaging of fluff and gossip as news may have been inevitable at CBS because of the lust of some stations, including one of its own, WCBS in New York, to mimic the perky pace and mindlessness of local TV news. It was more important to entertain your audience than to inform it.

"You Can Be Sure If It's Westinghouse…"

In my mind the steep road downhill for CBS News started when Laurence Tisch, a hotel, movie and tobacco company owner, took over the Tiffany network and began slashing jobs. Under Tisch, an atmosphere of fear prevailed at CBS, and its culture of excellence withered. Never think things can't get worse. Tisch was followed by Westinghouse, the refrigerator peddlers. The familiar slogan of the new owners could be recast as "You can be sure if it's Westinghouse it's all about money all the time." Quality was no longer part of the equation. Why pay an anchor $150,000 a year when you could find someone for $80,000? That's the way things were done at Westinghouse stations, and that's the way it should be done at the CBS Radio Networks.

The expertise and experience of an anchor that would be invaluable if you had to rush on the air with a sketchy but obviously very important story wasn't a big concern at Westinghouse. Although I had no idea what individual correspondents were paid by CBS, the thing that had always made CBS News so good, I thought, was a solid bench—a talented corps of smart, non-flashy journalists capable of handling any challenge. Mitchell Krauss, for example. A veteran reporter, who was slightly wounded during the assassination of Egyptian President Anwar Sadat, Mitchell was very adept at ad-libbing. If we had a single shred of information that I thought warranted getting on the air immediately, I would hope that Mitchell was around. He was well-informed, well-read and could fill time while waiting for reporters to talk to their sources or for the wire services to come up with a few details about the story, and he would do it smoothly without dispensing bullshit, nonsense or irresponsible speculation.

That wasn't the Westinghouse way. The less spent on anchors, editors, freelance reporters, technicians, overtime, and benefits the better. Everything about the ethos of Westinghouse rubbed me the wrong way. Soon after the takeover, I was at a meeting with an executive from WINS, a Westinghouse station, and recounted how well CBS News, Radio had done when Gene Kelly, the dancer-actor, died. (More to come about this.)

"What does Westinghouse do when big celebrities die?," I asked. "Do you have obits ready to go?"

"Nah," was the response. "We wait on the agencies to provide material."

It didn't seem to bother him that his station wouldn't be quick off the mark. How silly of me. To have a writer spend several hours putting an obit together on a major American personality would cost money and besides the most important thing was to get traffic and weather on the air on time. It made me really want to work for Westinghouse.

The business I stumbled into wasn't the business I stumbled out of. Having never done anything else, I had no way of comparing the changes in the news business to what was happening in other professions. If I had been a carpenter, hired by a firm with a reputation for using the best materials, employing the most skilled craftsmen and not leaving a job until things were as near perfect as possible, what would have been my reaction when the business was sold to people whose sole concern was how much money could be made and how fast expenses and personnel could be cut?

Suppose I stayed on under the new owners, and we were ordered to use cheap sheetrock instead of quality cement board as we always had before, to substitute plastic for metal wherever possible, and to not sweat making every joint, every beam fit tightly. If I did what the new bosses wanted, would I still be a carpenter? Or would I be something else even if I didn't know it or wouldn't admit it?

That question became more relevant than ever when CBS News, Radio introduced the iCast, a "newscast" for iPod users. In the first iCast, the anchor used the word "smart-ass," ridiculed Wal-Mart employees as well as a professor CBS News had interviewed, made at least two factual mistakes and suddenly set loose rock music in a "story" about Israeli shelling of Lebanon. Although it was pure madness, at least one TOM claimed the iCasts were a hit, were "loved." Maybe so, but like many love affairs it didn't last long. The iCast is no more, still it wouldn't surprise me if the devotees of show business came up with something even worse. Just give them time.

Long before CBS didn't renew my contract, I was certainly out of step with many TOMs in the radio industry. When I made speeches to news directors and GMs, I stressed that what made CBS News, Radio so different and special was the caliber of the writing of anchors such as David Jackson. I was wasting my time and theirs. Most of them didn't give a damn about writing. They wanted everything as short and sweet as possible. And LIVE. It didn't matter if a reporter had nothing to say, nothing to advance the story, or that whatever he did say was disjointed and clumsy. He was LIVE from the scene, and that's all that counted. He could have said LIVE and coast-to-coast, "I have the worst case of jock itch I've ever had, John. Back to you," and hardly anyone would have cared or noticed. The devotees of this style of radio "news" firmly believe that reporters or anchors shouldn't piddle around with too much context or get sidetracked by subtleties. Make it quick and dirty and LIVE and sign off.

It's common for the retirees in any profession to believe the "punks" who came after them don't know as much or work as hard. A former pressman for the New York *Daily News*, Frank Amato, has said of some of the younger guys working there, "They don't even know how to make a hat," referring to the caps pressman on the night shift traditionally made from old newspapers to keep ink out of their hair. Charles Oakley, formerly of the Chicago Bulls and the New York Knicks, was asked in a TV interview what he and former teammates Michael Jordan and Patrick Ewing talked about when they got together. "How bad the players are today," Oakley said, and he didn't look like he was kidding.

There isn't only one way to do the news, but material presented in a fast-paced format without attribution or context and packaged with a point of view isn't news nor is it fair and balanced. There are some very good journalists at commercial radio networks and stations today, but many of the TOMs who run things are in love with show business, fluff and buzz and have made it clear that's what better be on their air. Although it isn't funny, I chuckle when I think about those who are dispensing trash disguised as information today are likely to say about those who follow them: "They don't have any standards." No kidding. And who's fault is that?

Granted before the show business invasion, the rap on CBS Radio News was that it was stodgy, that the anchors sounded old, and that they loaded their broadcasts with stories of little, if any, immediate consequence to a U.S. audience. I don't vigorously dispute the part about story selection with regards to a few, (and yes) older anchors. But the pendulum later swung way too far in the other direction, driving away dedicated CBS listeners who expected serious news when they turned on their radios.

On September 11, 2001, Irene and I were driving home to Long Island from Maine and for six plus hours listened to CBS Radio's excellent coverage of the attack on America. It was calm, thorough, highly professional—Dan Raviv's anchor work was sensational—and carefully drew distinctions between what seemed to be known at any moment and what was still murky. Yet, as I argued in a letter to Andrew Heyward, then the CBS News president, can you expect a listener who genuinely cares about what is going on in the world to automatically flip on CBS to learn about something as frightening as an attack on the United States after he or she has been insulted, disappointed and frustrated so many previous times when various forms of junk were treated as leads? I think the natural temptation was to give up on CBS Radio and go elsewhere for news, both on ordinary and extraordinary days. The CBS-owned station in Boston, WBZ, has a strong signal in Maine, but had I known where to immediately find an NPR station that day I probably would have gone there first.

Months after writing to Heyward I read Pete Hamill's "News Is A Verb," and he made the point much better. "If the headlines scream about the living arrangements of the sitcom actress Ellen DeGeneres, what will they do if there is another Hiroshima?", Hamill asks.

For years those applying for jobs as radio writers at CBS News took a writing audition. In the post-Westinghouse times, a quiz on popular culture has been included. It's important to know, I gather, as much about Lady Gaga and Gym Class Heroes as it is the Shia and Sunnis in Iraq.

18

Sorry, AP, but $2 Doesn't Buy a Life-Time Friendship

The first check I received for being a crack newsman was from The Associated Press. It was for the handsome sum of $2 for phoning in details on a wreck in Anderson, Indiana, where I was working at WCBC. That left a good taste in my mouth that lasted for many years.

During my days at ABC, AP was generally considered more reliable than UPI, and Reuters was seen as being too British, too focused on news of interest to the Commonwealth nations. AP was printed on white teletype paper, UPI on yellow and Reuters on green. One ABC editor had a habit of nervously tearing off a small corner of AP and UPI copy and putting it in his mouth. I once asked if he would chew Reuters if it were printed on some color other than green. He wasn't much for tomfoolery and ignored me as I suppose he should have.

When I got to RFE, there was no AP copy. They refused to sell their wire to what they considered a propaganda agency. UPI and Reuters had no such restrictions. RFE had a fairly strict two-source rule, and sometimes an AP item published in *Stars and Stripes* or *The International Herald Tribune* provided that second source, and we could write the story, although the news was pretty stale by then.

Why not try to change that? With the approval of Jim Edwards, RFE's news director, I began calling the AP in Frankfurt whenever I spotted a good story we had only one source on and asked if they had it. If they did, we could go with our one source.

What was in it for AP? I tipped them off when their competitors had big news, including the morning Agence France Presse reported Russian tanks had suddenly appeared on the streets of Kabul. AFP was apparently first with the Russian invasion, and AP gave me a warm thank you when I relayed the word.

Just because we weren't subscribers to AP didn't mean the RFE desk didn't sneak a peek every once in a while at their wire, received (or more accurately purloined) via a radio link. It was supposed to be standard procedure, often forgotten, to make sure that whenever there were visitors to RFE's Central Newsroom someone ran over to the bank of wire machines that included Tass and the East European news agencies to turn off the AP machine and hide the copy.

My warm spot for The Associated Press and its product was badly damaged when I was hired by a company that relied on AP for much of its news. The TOMs at this place had struck a deal to get access to AP copy before other subscribers did and frequently before anyone at AP had seen the story outside of the person who wrote it and put it on the wire.

You shouldn't see the bride without makeup, and twenty-four hours a day we saw AP and all its warts. It's easy to pick on AP. They try to cover the world, and you can't always have the best people everywhere you need them, something I'm familiar with from my days at CBS News searching for overseas stringers.

But. Working at this outfit, you routinely got several versions of the same unedited AP story and some of them were beauts, e.g. copy from Guatemala one day that said "the brothers—four men and a woman." I wasn't the only one who at times thought the AP ought to be called the God damn AP or maybe even AP-OOPS.

If there were holes in a story, assumptions leaped to, officials misidentified by importance or rank, names dropped or misspelled, inconsistencies with previous stories on the subject, we had to try to make sense of it all. Our TOMs argued that access to the bulk of AP's copy before it had been edited gave us a leg up on the competition. Dogs are fond of having a leg up. At times we found ourselves with our legs spread wide apart.

We were encouraged to call AP when there were problems, say a discrepancy between the content in a BULLETIN and the wording used in the first three or four paragraphs of the item that followed. After many months of doing as instructed, I decided that unless it was a major story I would just throw away stuff from AP-OOPS that I didn't understand. Why waste my time? It was management that had put us in bed with AP, and it was the TOMs who should handle the phone calls and the sorting out. As the editor running the desk, you couldn't get bogged down in minor items that needed lots of work. There was so much material to look at you had to move on and tackle the pieces that did make sense and could be fashioned, it was to be hoped, into reasonable news stories.

A phone call to AP-OOPS was usually very unsatisfactory. A typical call went like this:

Me: "This is Larry McCoy at...I have a question about your latest story on Putin out of Moscow."

AP: "Hold on a second." Pause of thirty seconds to a minute during which I'm treated to an AP Radio newscast. "Okay, sorry. Who is this again?

Me: "This is Larry McCoy at...and I have some questions about your latest story on Putin."

AP: "A story on who?"

Me: "Putin. The Russian President."

AP: "Poland? (Pause.) Oh, Putin. Hold on let me transfer you." (Another pause and more of the AP Radio newscast) "This is Wayne. (I always seemed to end up with raspy, hapless Wayne.) May I help you?"

Me: "This is Larry McCoy of...and I have some questions about the latest Putin story out of Moscow."

AP: "What wire are you reading? The mumble-mumble wire or the garble-garble wire?"

Me: (Admittedly impatient.) "No idea. The story cleared at 15:38. My problem is that the lead says Putin promised to crack down on corruption and announced the firing of a deputy prime minister, but there are no quotes from Putin backing up the lead nor is the name of the person fired given anywhere."

AP: "Hmmm. You said 15:38? It's about Peru?"

Me: "Putin, Putin."

AP: "Oh, okay. What's your phone number?"

We had their phone number. They didn't have ours. Nice two-way street there. Every now and then you would get a call back and an explanation of something that had confused you when you first read it or you'd see a new story, eventually, that addressed the problems or a few of them. Or, and this was the least frequent but by far the most maddening, AP would send what it called a Corrective. Not a Correction. That was too damn straightforward.

Correction flat out conceded something was wrong. *The New York Times* did Corrections. The New Yorker did Corrections. The AP-OOPS did Correctives. "Corrective" is a softer, kinder word that keeps you from owning up to a mistake. Did anyone else use the word "corrective" besides AP and the orthopedic shoe business?

On rare, blissful occasions someone—perhaps a new hire assigned to a small bureau—would get all excited and correct something on the wire that was off the mark with a bell-ringing, clearly-labeled CORRECTION. I wonder if he got a swift email from New York saying we don't do that here. Corrections are a no-no. We hide our screwups under the corrective rubric, and we sleep better at night, have harder abs and tighter buns because of it. To me, Correctives smacked of something you expect from a government-run news agency dedicated to concealing the truth.

19

"CNN Can Now Confirm...."

*A*lthough not a religious person, I was a witness every couple of weeks to a miracle. The process often began with *The New York Times* or *The Washington Post* publishing a carefully-worded story pinned on "usually reliable sources" or perhaps "sources who attended the meetings but weren't authorized to talk about them."

The story got picked up by broadcast and cable networks with the information clearly attributed, most times, to *The Times* or *The Post* with the sourcing close or identical to the wording in the newspaper.

"The New York Times is reporting this morning that usually reliable sources at the Pentagon say the President has been told the U.S. and its allies have only about six months to get things right in Iraq or they could face the prospect of all-out civil war."

So far, so fine. What appeared to be a good story was picked up by other news outfits and properly attributed to the paper that dug it up.

As the day wore on, and anchors, writers and reporters moved into their third or fourth retelling of the story, things loosened up. An hour or so after the news first broke the "usually reliable sources at the Pentagon" were simply "sources" and the scoop in *The New York Times* was now merely "a published report." What was being reporting was often changing too. Where, for example, the newspaper's editors and reporters chose the word "could" in their lead—"could face the prospect of all-out civil war"—a few of the live shot ad-libbers on TV sloppily converted this into a "would" or a "will."

The cable networks summoned the hired throats—the ex-generals and colonels, the wannabes of the State Department and the political consultants—and they talked and talked and talked about the story, which now was seldom referred to as a report developed with the help of "usually reliable sources" but was presented as fact, as the truth, as gospel. At some point in this progression, CNN, for instance, would say, "CNN can now confirm" what *The Times* reported. That came about two hours after the original story was published.

Was this not a miracle? A piece that a reporter or maybe two or three reporters spent weeks crafting for their newspaper, a story that perhaps the editors held for several days hoping to get more specifics before publishing it, that story was soon on all the cable news networks and probably the wire services too. What took the newspaper so long in getting it if the cable nets and wire services could track that sucker down so quickly?

Good question. Competent beat reporters at the Pentagon would, it is hoped, have called their sources about *The Times* report. Now that it was in the news these sources could be more willing to provide some "guidance," maybe supplying additional tidbits or cautioning about aspects of the published version they felt were wrong or overblown. However, all too many times the TV or radio reporters parroting the original piece didn't cover the beat involved — the Pentagon in our make-believe case — and had already been lined up the day before to do live shots outside the White House or in a studio on whatever was considered hot news the next morning. Here they were live, and in living color on TV, spouting off on a story that wasn't theirs from a beat that also wasn't theirs. Journalism. It makes you proud, doesn't it?

"It's on the Wires."

A truly strange thing about radio and television newsrooms was that they were scared of themselves. Even editors and writers who had been in broadcasting for years had less trust in something they heard or saw than they did in something in print. They were slaves to the wires. In his book "Arrogance," former CBS News correspondent Bernard Goldberg tells of the Los Angeles bureau manager calling the radio desk in New York to give an eyewitness account of an earthquake he had just experienced. The first reaction from an editor was to see if there was anything about it on the wires. The bureau manager's account wasn't broadcast until the wires caught up with the story. When it "did hit the wires, it became real news," Goldberg writes.

Years after that incident Ronnie Bradford, the assignment editor at KNX, the CBS radio station in Los Angeles, passed along a tip to me that Gene Kelly had died along with a phone number for Kelly's agent. I got lucky, at least in a newsman's sense of lucky. The agent confirmed that Kelly was dead and gave a few details about who was with the dancer-actor at the time. We quickly did a Special Report, using a taped obituary we had ready.

We were way ahead. AP's first word on Kelly's death was a brief item attributed to us. It was a good twenty minutes before AP and Reuters got their own stories, and the second they appeared there was nervous chatter in the newsroom. "It's on the wires" was repeated over and over, with an obvious sense of relief. It was now in print and consequently now believable.

This would be a good time to quote the Lord's Prayer, at least the passage about "lead us not into temptation." Doing what the competition was doing was THE temptation in news. It was hellishly hard to resist. Network folks got uneasy when they saw or heard that a competitor had a story or certain pictures on the air. The TV evening news producers would sometimes change their lead, move a story up much higher in the lineup or add a story after watching what a competitor did on its first feed at six-thirty p.m. Eastern time.

On retiring several years ago a producer from a TV special events unit — the people who decide when there is news big enough to interrupt network programming with a Special Report — reminisced in a farewell note about "all that OJ and Michael Jackson crap, and all those bizarre 'double chicken' games, waiting to see if the other nets would force us on the air."

What's this? Networks send SWAT teams into a competitor's control room to demand that the network get on the air immediately or they would start shooting? Not quite. For whatever reason — possibilities include not trusting their own judgment along with an uncomfortable feeling that most people are smarter than they are — top news producers, star anchors, network executives, and network affiliates, particularly the affiliates—didn't like the competition to be on the air when their network wasn't.

The fact that the competition's anchors or reporters were struggling to find words to convey an essentially worthless story doesn't come close to being a persuasive rebuttal. They're on the air and we're not and that's all that mattered. Logic is not always a highly valued gift in the news biz. When a network, usually one of the cable outfits, jumped on the air after a competitor had and both then spun their wheels on a really nothing story, it made you hope that one of the networks would be honest enough one day to rename itself SBS, the Sheep Broadcasting System.

Like most people, broadcast journalists find it harder to resist temptation the later it gets. You have air time to fill and how are you going to do it? On a very slow Sunday night at CBS, I stood at a tape machine, listening to sound bites and correspondents' reports trying to find something worthwhile to use on the next newscast. Nothing I heard was newsy or appealing, and I said to a lady writer standing near me, "You know, tape is like a woman. The later it gets, the better it looks." Sexist? Probably. Ok, it was sexist. It also was true. Unless you were careful your editorial standards tended to decline as the day wore on, especially on a dull news day. The closer you were to going home the more you had to guard against airing a badly-written, pathetic, weakly-sourced piece from a freelancer in Ost Obernsdorf, Germany, merely because it hadn't been used before and because you were in a hurry to get your last broadcast over and head out the door.

It's the same temptation that faced news staffs as they re-wrote and re-packaged, for the fifth time, that solid story in *The New York Times* about "usually reliable sources at the Pentagon." Network newsrooms should invest in big neon signs that read "Lead us not into temptation but deliver us from evil," mount them on the wall facing the copy desk and rig them so they begin flashing two hours before every shift change. It would be money well-invested.

20

"...in Tennessee of All Places."

There's no reason to be bashful when you hear something on the air that strikes you as ridiculous, out of bounds, small-minded or all three. Don't dawdle. Fire off a note right away. After a November 1998 broadcast of "48 Hours," I sent a letter to Susan Zirinsky, the executive producer of the CBS News program.

Dear Susan,

Did you ever wonder what would get on the air — both story selection and language — if one of the broadcast networks had set up its headquarters in Grand Rapids or Sioux Falls? I have. Many times.

As someone who grew up in Indiana, it's aggravating and disappointing to listen daily to so many otherwise intelligent network correspondents be so damn condescending when dealing with people who aren't from one of the coasts. On last night's '48 Hours,' Cynthia Bowers talked in apparent amazement about 'a nice, simple country boy.' The assumption seems to be that if you are not from the city you're not smart. Should you be from the country and do something smart then the Vatican should be notified because it's a miracle.

Tennessee is a state which produced Cordell Hull as well as Dolly Parton yet Bowers said on the air: 'In Tennessee of all places.' It's like saying, 'Gee, Judy, you did real well. For a girl.'

This sort of big city elitism is not confined to the networks. The Times had a headline the other day saying the Varga Girl paintings might not be considered art, but they are 'in Kansas.' And Lenore Skenazy of the (New York) Daily News said in a column that 'manure is the chewing gum of Iowa.' I guess she was trying to be funny. What she was was provincial.

The best journalist I ever met left school after the eighth grade. He speaks three languages and writes in two of them. Maybe if Andrew [Heyward, the president of CBS News at the time] can't move the operation to Grand Rapids or Sioux Falls, he should order that no one be hired as a correspondent who went beyond the eighth grade.

Regards and say hello to Joe [Peyronnin, her husband, who is also a journalist],

Larry McCoy

At a bar a couple of months later, I saw Zirinsky, who had always been very supportive of radio, and asked if she had seen my letter. It didn't ring a bell. Maybe an assistant intercepted it, thought it was nonsense and threw it away. But tenacity is one of the better traits of many of us from the Midwest, so we keep pushing our fervent conviction that, while the Big Apple is exciting, wonderful and impressive, it isn't the only place on earth where people can live happy, very successful lives. I voiced those sentiments in a note written for a memorial service in 2002 for Vicki Kelley, a splendid export from the Midwest who was an anchor for CBS News and later "The Wall Street Journal Report."

Although we never talked about it, I suspect one big reason Vicki and I hit it off was that we were both from the Midwest. She was from Illinois, I'm from Indiana. Granted that it's a deep prejudice of mine, but those of us who grew up in small towns in the Midwest become missionaries when we get to the big city. We have to because many of the people raised here don't know a thing. Not a blessed thing. One of my landladies on Long Island could never quite grasp the concept of Indiana and where it was. She once asked if it was on the way to Florida.

Several years ago at CBS News a big city person working in a tape room was asked to call South Dakota or Montana where the snow was so bad they were helicoptering cattle to safety. The city person in the tape room asked the National Guard spokesman, 'How many cows can you get in a helicopter?' (For you city folk, the cows don't ride in the helicopters. Crews put a belt around them and carry them to safety.)

There IS a magic about this place though. They don't call it the Big Apple for nothing. And it's certainly the Big Time in broadcasting....

Once Vicki got behind the big network mike in the big city she knew what to do. Unlike some others with bigger salaries, bigger egos — who ever heard of big egos in broadcasting? — better hours and, not to mention, better clothes, she kept up on what was going on. She knew what was news, and, unlike many others, she actually understood what she was saying on the air. What a concept!

Nothing threw her. Late copy, late tape, no tape, mumbled instructions from editors or managers, conflicting accounts two minutes to air from two reporters supposedly covering the same story. It didn't matter. She could handle it. One day she could report from a Farm Aid concert in Illinois and a day later, back in New York, write four fine sentences on the SALT talks in Austria. She cared about the news and the words used to tell it, and listeners as well as managers knew it.

With everything that was going on in her life [a wrenching divorce], I never heard Vicki complain. She did, however, occasionally wonder out loud in my presence if the management of CBS News, Radio truly understood the feeling an anchor has on the overnight shift when, three minutes before her next broadcast, she has been assigned no tape and is the ONLY one in the newsroom. Both the copy and assignment editors have disappeared and even the desk assistant is nowhere in sight. I always gave her the old management 'uh huh, uh huh' and promised to look into it.

For my money, one of the highlights of her time at CBS News was the night she spent with Doug Poling. Hurricane Hugo was pounding the hell out of South Carolina, and she had put in a long day doing Updates on the storm. She asked about the chances of going home, and, like a good manager, I suggested, 'Ah, just a couple more.' Seconds later Poling somehow got a phone line through to New York and did an exceptional on-scener outside Charleston city hall. Vicki got her second wind and refused to leave — she just kept doing Update after Update, hour after hour. That was Vicki. She cared, really cared.

She was also always great fun to work with, something that certainly can't be said about everyone in broadcasting. Even on the 'baddest' of her days, she never lost that marvelous sense of humor.

Vicki Kelley was truly special. It was an honor to have worked with her. Everyone liked her and respected her. She was a wonderful person, a terrific journalist and, best of all, one fine missionary.

I should have added that Vicki did pretty damn well in Manhattan, of all places. (I arrived late for the service and never made the remarks, though I passed them on to Vicki's family.)

21

Challenge Co-Workers on the Job Not on the Court

If you ever get the temptation to invite everyone at work to a game of basketball (or tennis or handball or whatever) with drinks and food afterward at your house, don't. Trust me. It's an awful idea.

While at ABC News, I got up early many mornings to play basketball before heading to Manhattan. I climbed a fence at a park in Long Beach, New York, and shot around for half an hour before showering and eating breakfast. At the office, I couldn't stop blowing off about it.

Somehow I got the really super idea of inviting the entire radio staff to my house for a day of basketball, beer and fried chicken. I wrote a note challenging anyone and everyone to come out on a Saturday afternoon, closing my classy invitation with the line: "everyone is invited, except Dick Aronson."

See where this is going? I fried a ton of chicken, bought side dishes and many, many cold beers. (Irene, always the wiser partner in the marriage, found "things to do" with the kids that day and was out.) The first person to arrive was Dick Aronson. He was also the only person to arrive.

Dick, a tech and a delightful human being, lived 20 minutes away. No one else called me or left "sorry, can't make it" messages in my mailbox at work. I liked Dick, but he didn't play basketball and if he did it wouldn't have been pretty. We had some beers, some chicken and some conversation. After an hour or so, he went home. It had to be one of the most embarrassing days in the life of a big mouth.

I don't look back on this as a funny, goofy memory. You can't expect others to share your passions, whether it's doing your damnedest to tell a story clearly and succinctly or working up a good sweat on a basketball court. My invite for a day of basketball was plain, flat ass dumb. What would you expect from a future TOM ? Serves me right.

22

What They Should Teach in Journalism School

You know you picked the right profession when you're sitting at lunch in the house tavern with the wife of one of your bosses, and she says, "I'm not wearing any underwear." True, you should never take advantage of a lady who has sipped too much alcohol, then again "never" is a long time and life is short, right?

I worked with several good newshounds who later taught journalism, but I doubt that any of their courses dealt with how a beginner, or a veteran for that matter, should respond when told "I'm not wearing any underwear." With college costs what they are, shouldn't kids expect their professors to pass on some snappy retorts to such a declaration?

"Me neither," could be one.

Or "Ya wanna wear mine for a while?"

Or "That's the way I like my women AND boys."

I know I had no witty comeback ready. At best, I nodded or harrumphed. I had to get back across the street where the lady's husband had undoubtedly worked through his lunch hour. Based on the hours he kept, they probably saw little of each other, with or without their underwear on, and that may have been part of the reason she was a little loaded and hanging out at the company pub.

I don't read scholarly books on any subject, certainly not on journalism, but I'd bet my house there is one phenomenon that no journalism school or any advanced academic program has ever studied in depth. In the pre-smartphone era, how was it that when food, especially cake, was brought into the newsroom to mark someone's last day (at work, not on earth) or to celebrate an accomplishment by an employee or a unit, the news spread instantly to others in the company scattered throughout the building? This signaling system, or whatever it was, was ten times quicker and more efficient than the Internet will ever be.

When the word went out at CBS that "there's cake in radio," people you might have seen in the hallway or in the john but had never had any dealings with were suddenly standing next to you with a paper plate sagging from a gigantic slab of chocolate cake. What was the scientific or mathematical explanation for this? And as soon as the interlopers had snatched a piece of cake, a couple of Danish, or whatever goodies there were to be had, they disappeared. Gone. Not to be seen again until the next coming of food.

This mystery, I say, cried for investigation and thorough study. It's probably too late now.

I also wonder whether those paying their money to J schools are being clued in on the proper way to exit a newsroom after a dispute with a boss. One shortcoming of RFE was that the house tavern was just a floor below the newsroom. The cafeteria in the basement served alcoholic refreshments, perhaps my favorite oxymoron. When the cafeteria was closed, beer was available in a vending machine. As we saw a while back, one gentleman consumed a quantity of liquids on RFE's premises one evening before pouring a container of coffee and brandy on my head and jumping out the window.

I could be very rude and obscene in a newsroom and that lack of a charming disposition, coupled with my work habits, convinced some people that I was not only abnormal but a Grade A son of a bitch. When running the night desk at RFE, I didn't take a dinner break, figuring there was too much work to do. To some I was a pathetic workaholic in the land of boisterous beer halls. More than thirty years after I left RFE there are still those who feel that way. An Australian (not the window jumper) said in an email that I had been too intense back then, didn't know how to relax and have fun. Enjoying yourself at work is one thing, relaxing on the job strikes me as unprofessional, an invitation to mistakes.

To my mind, any journalism school worth a damn should require students to take courses in:

(1) Working amiably with demanding sons of bitches who never abandon their desks in search of food.

(2) Graceful, safe egress from company property after a run-in with one of those SOBs. This course could be called Look Before You Leap.

(3) How to react, including tips on avoiding unnecessary eye contact, when you hear a member of one of the four sexes say, "I'm not wearing any underwear."

Without such courses, how are J schools preparing their students for the real world?

Judging by ads I've seen, the ideal candidate for a tenure track position at a journalism school is someone who has spent many years in classrooms working on a PhD and seventeen days one summer in an honest to God newsroom in Keokuk. Is this not totally backasswards?

All that time in class eats away at your mind. Here's a little ditty received in the mail from the "Director of the School of Communication" at a major Midwest university.

"For the past two summers, we have taken an entrepreneurial approach to summer classes offered: those classes that go beyond enrollment cost minimums are offered to support those that are more expensive to deliver. Plus, revenue received beyond cost of class delivery has been used to support faculty travel so we can maintain our professional and scholarly leadership at national and international levels and in renovating former photography darkrooms to create a professional environment for our 40 graduate teaching assistants. This space became available when we moved to digital photography."

And this space is being left available (_____) for an English translation of that twaddle. Can you imagine having lunch with anyone who churns out bilge like that? What would you say if this person sprung on you the fact that he wasn't wearing any underwear?

Hello, Journalism Departments, get with it! Not only do you need to prepare your students for life outside the classroom, you might want to devote a bit of time to seeing if you can teach your faculty members how to write.

23

Bullshit is One Word, Performance Review Two

*A*fter leaving CBS, I loafed for a year and then spent several years working as a copy editor. Shortly after arriving at the office one day, a manager came over to my desk and declared, "We need to discuss your goals." I was sixty-six years old — past retirement age, damn near old enough to be his father — and he wants to discuss my "goals."

"Go away," I told him. Preparing to take over the main desk was always a hectic part of the day. I was reading in, looking at the stories the desk had edited that day. So much ground to cover, so little time. It was impossible to read every story from start to finish, so you skimmed some, skipped some but made sure you thoroughly read the big ones, the ones you knew would be changing throughout your shift.

Floyd was a TOM and wasn't attuned to the idea of a right time and place to do things. Like a squirrel digging for nuts, Floyd kept at it. "We have to discuss your goals sometime. It's part of your Performance Review."

"Well, we're not doing it now. Go away!"

Floyd was both dense and tone deaf. He wouldn't leave. If only Floyd were as dogged in fleshing out a good story. The Performance Review had to be done, he said. I wasn't going to budge either. It was a crock — something dreamed up by the stiffs in human resources who had nothing to do and, worst of all, absolutely no experience in newsrooms. They all ought to be fired, I told Floyd, several times in several ways. This back and forth continued, with the volume of each exchange rising, until the magic words came out.

"Go fuck yourself," I said.

Why does anyone say that? It's a physical impossibility for most of us, isn't it? It has to be or otherwise every country in the world would have a jobless rate of over ninety-eight percent because most everyone would be home—fucking themselves.

Floyd reddened—a condition associated with self-fucking—and accused me of being incapable of a civil conversation and suggested it was time to retire. Then the squirrel left without finding his nuts. Perhaps he went looking for them elsewhere. He didn't come in for the next two or three days.

I concede I was out of line, but if he felt he had a chore to do—and I'm sure he did—then there had to be a better way to alert an editor about to take charge of the desk that sometime soon they needed to set a time for the two of them to sit down and talk about the Performance Review. The next time Floyd showed up a date was agreed on.

We met in the conference room with its breathtaking view of parking garages, and, while I was admiring the scene, Floyd handed me the damn thing and said my overall rating wasn't just his opinion but the collective judgment of every TOM in the unit. After only a glance at a couple of pages, I let him have it. My editorial skills got the highest possible marks, fives, but right below those was a two and the word "outbursts." In the language of the TOMs, "Larry must control his outbursts." Hello? If you "control" an "outburst," it isn't an "outburst." It's whining.

A second two caught my eye. "Larry must work on his people skills."

"You think everything's fine here, don't you. If I'd just shut up, things would be perfect."

Floyd was quick with a "No, no. We value your judgment and want you to point out problems but try…."

"Bullshit. You want a newsroom full of wusses. You don't want to hear it when one of our reporters or AP butchers a story or misses the point completely. And it happens all the time, all the God damn time."

"That's not true," Floyd said, reddening again. Was he doing himself again? If so it wasn't my fault.

I began a running commentary on a few of the other evaluations.

"Listen to this: 'Invests time in developing and coaching staff.' And I get a three. That's not my job. That's your job! According to this piece of shit you gave me, I'm supposed to do your job and then you call me in and tell me how well I'm doing, doing your job. Right? That's insane."

An anxious chirp was all I got from Floyd whose eyes looked glazed. Not surprising, if he took the least bit of this foolishness seriously.

"And how about this one? 'Moves others to action without a reliance on positional authority or proximity. Builds consensus through give-and-take, and facilitates win-win business outcomes.' What the hell does that mean? I don't understand a word of it."

"Well, yes, that is a muddle, isn't it," he snorted while shaking his legs.

"What the fuck does it mean?"

"I don't know either, frankly. Some of this language is standard to all departments and comes down from the human resources people," Floyd said.

"Ahhh. You inherit language from someone else, give me a grade on it and then admit you don't know what it means. That's one hell of a wonderful system."

I was worse than he was. I was digging for nuts, his.

"Here's another good one, Fuh-LOYD. I get a two for 'Keeps supervisor appropriately informed.' Isn't it the supervisor's job to keep up, to know what's going on? Why would any intelligent journalist tell a supervisor here what was going on? The one sure way to make sure something doesn't get done quickly or doesn't get corrected is to tell a supervisor about it like I stupidly did the day Dale Evans died. AP called her 'Queen of the Cowgirls,' so of course that's what we called her instead of 'Queen of the West.' We had it wrong, but management claimed there was no need for a correction. Why not? It wasn't wrong enough?"

I could have gone on for days, but it was like yelling at a four-year-old for wetting his pants: even if you have a point, it doesn't help the situation. "If we're done here, I'd like to finish reading in and get on the desk."

Floyd nodded, tried to smile and pointed to the box where

my signature went to acknowledge that he and I had discussed my Performance Review, but, of course, not his performance. I actually felt sorry for him. Imagine, a grown man being told to waste time on such crap.

Later that evening, after all the TOMs had gone, Wally, my favorite person in the newsroom because he frequently was the only one on the rewrite bank who had any clue what to do with an important but confusing story, asked how the Performance Review had gone. Although I had a feeling he already knew about my "go fuck yourself" comment, I told him about it anyway. It was only then that I realized Floyd and I had never discussed my goals. What were my goals outside of trying to do a good job and finding good stories and interesting angles others may have overlooked?

Wally, who is at least ten years younger than I am, said Floyd had approached him earlier in the week about his Performance Review and the need to discuss his goals.

"What did you tell him?" I asked.

"World peace."

I laughed. "World peace is your goal. I like that. I'll remember it for next time."

"Yeah, when he asks you, you can tell him, 'World peace. Now go fuck yourself.'"

24

Give Me That Old-Time Newsroom, it's Good Enough for Me

Newsrooms certainly changed over the four-and-a-half decades I was in them and not all the changes were that brilliant. Yes, we smoked a lot at our desks in the old days and that's neither smart nor good for you. Yes, many of us drank too much in the '60s, '70s and '80s and that's not too bright or healthy either. Yes, the horseplay could get out of hand—a cherry bomb thrown under the editor's desk and a starter's pistol fired at a producer as a "joke" at ABC Radio are two egregious examples. But amid the smoke and the pain from hangovers and the occasional mindless lapses, there was a life, a vibrancy, an energy that simply didn't exist the last time I was in a newsroom.

The political correctness zombies made newsrooms much less interesting and, at times, much less competent. It wasn't nice to raise your voice or swear or have a tantrum or even an "outburst" when something went wrong, when someone genuinely dropped the ball. This wasn't the way I was brought up. Weren't you supposed to care? Weren't writers, editors, anchors and managers supposed to be upset and maybe even furious if a story got fouled up? And how were you expected to express your disappointment and frustration that things went down the tubes? With a smile and a hug and a verbal pat on the back?

"Gee, Max, those are nice slacks. Too bad we said it was the president of France killed in that car wreck in Cannes. Next time around please be sure to say it was the president's brother."

No, thank you. A serious mistake should leave a journalist in agony. I always thought a TOM should tell someone when they fell way short, either face-to-face or in a memo or both. That's now considered old school. Late one afternoon an editor spotted an item on a website and misread or misunderstood something buried at the bottom of it and turned that perceived gem into the lead to a story. He had it all wrong. He had reached a conclusion not justified by the material on the website, his sole source for the piece. When a TOM, a very likeable manager, was alerted to the problem, he stayed late to handle the correction.

The next time we saw each other I asked if he had spoken to the editor about the mistake. No, I was told. I was astounded. Why not? When an editor does a sloppy job and no one in management points it out to him, isn't it likely that there will be other instances of mangled interpretation of what the news is? TOMs aren't supposed to be afraid of subordinates or reluctant to tell them when they produce something shoddy, are they?

No one is clearly in command in some newsrooms now and that includes places swamped with managers. Too many TOMs automatically creates too much turf, and the more fiefdoms there are the harder it is for quick decisions to be made. Some newsrooms apparently think all opinions are equal. At least one all-news station held a staff meeting to vote on what stories to do. That seems to me a formula for assuring that the station does only the same type of stories it's always done, does them the same way and holds them to the same length. Someone has to be in charge, to give orders, to make decisions. Newsrooms aren't democracies or at least good ones aren't.

My most uncomfortable night in news was a result of confusion about who was running things. I was the night copy editor at ABC Radio on January 27, 1967 when there was a fire on a launch pad at Cape Kennedy. The managing editor, who had a habit of hanging around the office in the evening, surprised me by stepping in to co-anchor our live coverage. Normally he did very little air work, and in addition to anchoring that night he was still functioning as managing editor, giving instructions to the staff, but not me, on what he wanted done. I didn't know what was going on or what I should do. I should have either taken charge or had a quick talk with the managing editor-anchor about how I could fit in the mix. I didn't. I think ABC's coverage of the death of the three astronauts (news that NASA took its time in disclosing) could have been much sharper if one person had been in control, clearly deciding what we were chasing and putting on the air.

Among the lunacies that have become standard business practice today is the refusal to grade former employees when a potential new employer calls. You confirm that Joe the Jerk took up space in your newsroom for five years, but because of lawyers and the twits in human resources you are forbidden to tell the person inquiring about Joe the Jerk that he certainly earned his nickname or that, despite that moniker, they don't come any better than Joe. This strikes me as particularly inane and unprofessional in a business supposedly dedicated to dispensing solid information and informed opinion.

If you don't think political correctness sucked much of the air out of many newsrooms, another example. As an old guy, I reported to TOMs who were young enough, in some cases, to be my kids. (I'm certain they're glad they weren't.) Arriving for work one day, I gave an old-style salutation to an aging journeyman, a description I use with affection because I like the guy both as a journalist and as a person. He is permanently disheveled from scalp to toes. On this particular day his hair seemed especially messy, so I greeted him by saying, "Your barber called." He quickly returned the compliment, "Your mortician called." It was our way of saying hello, an expression of fondness. Two old guys who like each other prefer to begin their day with some version of "go fuck yourself" rather than exchanging the dull, meaningless, "Hello, how are you?"

A few days after these pleasantries the journeyman was called in for his Performance Review, and one of the TOMs said, "You and Larry don't get along, I hear." The TOM had been told about our exchange. The journeyman made clear to the TOMs that wasn't true and mentioned their comments to me.

I (surprise) wrote a note, informing the TOMs the two of us were pals, both personally and professionally, who had our own ways of starting the business day. Among my suggestions was that the young managers loosen up and stop being so damn serious. Geez!

"She Taught Me How to Do My Sock Drawer."

After one extremely frustrating day, I turned on my home computer and wrote to someone I had known for years, going through a litany of gripes about what had happened to the business we had been in since we were kids. Greg is a lover of cheap cigars and a social conservative, though I always thought he deliberately came off sounding more right wing than he really was. My note played to many of the stereotypes about a cigar-smoking Republican.

Dear Greg,

I think you can trace it all back to when these rich white women started agitating to bring their daughters to work one day a year, so 'they can see what mommy does.' You're right. These were all mommies with pretty decent white-collar jobs, not ladies cleaning the toilets at Rockefeller Center at night.

This was one of the first waves of this political correctness horseshit, and for my money newsrooms soon went straight to hell. Nowadays you can't tell a joke about a blonde bimbo who gets into a boat with a Jew, a WASP and a big black farmer with red radishes sticking out of his pockets. Forget the jokes about the Italians, the ones you could tell with a real heavy accent. The PC Nazis are all over the place. The bastards have taken over.

Now that they're king of the hill in newsrooms you can't tell a decent joke, but you can sit there watching the telly in between assignments and see two guys give each other some tongue. Progress, hey?

And the people they're hiring, forget it. None of them come in hung-over, none of them talk about getting laid or getting drunk or getting laid while drunk. Not a word. Some lollygagger who used to sit near me said out loud — I shit you not — the day Martha Stewart was convicted, 'Oh, no. She taught me how to do my sock drawer.' He was never more serious.

Just when you might have thought there wasn't a God, this cucumber soon moved on to Boise and out of my sight where at this very moment he's rearranging his sock drawer. Don't forget, Buster, argyles to the left, tube socks to the right.

Remember the days when desk assistants didn't have attitude but willingly made a trip every hour down to the cafeteria to get coffee and food? Gone, of course. The rat hole I'm in now doesn't even have any one to answer the phones, and every lame brain on the payroll calls the main news desk and asks to be transferred. Guess what I tell these pantywaists? Guess whether I transfer them? Their brains are so small they can remember only one number with more than two digits and that one number rings on my desk. Figures.

Amid all this carping you might like to know something you used to say has been passed on to another generation. I remember when we were in newsrooms together, and if you heard some foreign leader rattle off something in Spanish, German or French you'd always say, 'You do and you'll clean it up.' My grandson thinks that's one of the funniest things he's ever heard and uses it himself now and then.

All this brings me to the lead, which, in keeping with the new journalism, I have buried. It isn't only newsrooms that have been tampered and messed with to the detriment of all. There is this place where I stop every bloody morning to get a coffee and a dollar lottery scratch-off before I get on the train. It's run by Indians. No, not Chief Running Thunder, the other kind—Nehru, Gandhi, curry people. Recently they have gussied the place up a bit and now in addition to newspapers, dirty magazines, coffee, cigarettes, cigars, candy and lottery tickets, they're selling water, Snapple and juices and all that yuppy crapola. And they've hired another Indian who keeps all the shelves stocked. The other day, as I was paying for my coffee and lottery ticket, the chief Indian says something in Hindi to the stock shelf Indian, and I say, 'I told him the same thing yesterday. He doesn't listen.' The chief Indian smiled, which is better than nothing in these rush-rush days.

It was then that I saw them, Greg. Behind the counter there were these green and peach-colored boxes. Cigars. WHITE OWLS! Your old favorites. And would you like to bet your big white ass what kind of White Owls they were? The green one was Wild Apple

White Owls and the peach one was, yes sirree, Peach White Owls. Doesn't that make you want to grab your box and just go bananas? Well, it sure does me. Would you please stop fucking around with White Owls, you dimwitted-short-toed toads!

I'm thinking of putting a brick in my briefcase and going in there someday and destroying that display. Better yet, I might try to stand on a big stack of *The New York Times* and see if I can urinate all the way over to the White Owls. But to be honest the way things are going these days, I'd better settle for a brick.

I have to close. I heard an alarm go off. Most likely it's time for my medication, the big yellow mother of a pill I take twice a day. Hope all's well on your end, so to speak. Both ends for that matter. And try to do a better job of reading the paper before you get to work, okay?

Cheers,

Larry

I didn't, for once, mail this diatribe. Yes, it's over the top, still there are kernels of truth too, me thinks.

25

"This is the Only Place I've Ever Worked Where...."

Let me tell you what managers really like. They like notes, smart-ass notes that begin with "This is the only place I've ever worked where...." That sort of cheerful opening line leaves a manager tingling from the chin to the crotch, or, depending on how often the big guy or big gal gets to the gym, from the chins to the crotches.

It really turns them off, these comparisons to past employers because they know damn well that four long years removed from your last hideous job you now imagine things ran smoothly there. Managers say to themselves—and if you've written a truly successful note, one that has really pissed them off—they may say it to your face, "If the *New Haven Digital Probe And News* was all that great, why did you leave?" Whatever legitimate problem, travesty, grievance, lunacy you wanted to bring to their attention in your note doesn't matter. They aren't listening.

That, however, doesn't stop a few of us from writing "this is the only place" missives and, at least in my case, not only writing them but sending them. I recommend that notes to TOMs be written late in the day, after a bourbon or drink of your choice, that they be composed via feverish pounding of the keyboard, that they be read and re-read four or five times for mistakes in grammar, spelling, punctuation and perhaps even logic and then, after you have given it one final look and the thought flashes through your mind that you'd better not send this, you say the hell with it and hit the send button. You'll feel terrific afterward. Lean back and smile. Relax. It won't be the end of the world.

What bosses like best of all is for you to write a note to THEIR boss. When firing off a few lines to my boss's boss, I ignored the long ago warnings of a station owner in Bedford, Indiana, and utilized that powerful tool known as sarcasm. If properly employed by an experienced practitioner, sarcasm can elevate a note to the boss's boss to Super Bowl heights.

Going over the head of your immediate boss brings immediate action. Not to your complaints about personnel or procedures in the shop, but rather phone calls, emails and many meetings among the TOMs regarding you and questions about what will be characterized as your "stability."

When it was decreed at one news outlet that SpellCheck was to be deleted from the computers, a few of us objected on the grounds that we were being deprived of a tool we relied upon. Yes, SpellCheck doesn't catch every misspelling, and it can butcher people's names. (If you don't believe me, ask Eliot Spitfire.) Still, I and others found SpellCheck valuable, particularly when we were the only person on duty and it was our sole backstop to catch misspellings.

Following my own syllabus on note writing—late in the day, bourbon in belly, heavy beating on keyboard—I launched one up into the ether to the boss of my boss, protesting the end of SpellCheck. In a clever twist, mi noat wuz loded wit mizpeled wurds.

Let's pretend that my boss's boss was a guy named Jim. My letter began "Deer Gym" and went uphil ore downhil vrom their:

> "Wen Eye got inntwo thiss bizness fourtee ears agoh @youpeeeye Eye wuz tolled wee were xpected two spel wordz write. Noww thanke Gott, Eye'm beeing tolled two furget abut itt. Nowl maybee Eye kan finnish moar storees befour Eye goh hoam.
> "Sinncerelee,
> "Larrrrrrrrrrrrrrrrrrry Mcoy
> "P.S. In over 40 years in newsrooms this ukase ranks as the most baffling and depressing!"

I felt so strongly about the matter that I emailed copies to every manager in my section of the newsroom. It would be a slight understatement to say that my immediate boss went nuts. Emails were sent to my home and work computers, instructing me to see him the minute I arrived in the office.

It was a brief, unpleasant session. I repeated my contention that the TOMs apparently didn't care about accuracy if they had eliminated a computer function that helped catch misspellings, especially by those of us who weren't good proofreaders of our own copy. I was told I was out of line, that I had to stop sending late night emails, had to stop ridiculing fellow workers as well as my many bosses. (If you can't do that, what's there to live for?) The validity of my argument wasn't addressed. I had crossed the line. Even if I were right, my tone was wrong or that's what I concluded from the icy meeting.

Another element of an endearing note to a boss can be a reference to the money paid to managers. Because the actual amount that goes into their bank accounts is none of your business, push your argument to a higher plane, to one that wonders out loud whether the shareholders are getting their money's worth. The watchdog strategy.

Near the end of my time in newsrooms, the TOMs fell in love with the word "permission." If there was an item on AP-OOPs or on a website that a beat reporter at the Pentagon or White House hadn't done, a desk person might ask whether our folks were planning to do it. In such a scenario, a TOM would come over to the desk and quietly say we had "permission" (from the reporter) to do the story.

Isn't "permission" something you last asked for in grade school when you had to go pee-pee? Well, being told we had "permission" to do story X frosted me and my pajamas real good. Note time! I composed a short email to the managers. If reporters were running the newsroom with powers of decision over the stories we did and if changing more than one word of their sacred copy required an act of Congress, then why were managers needed? Wouldn't a lot of shareholder money be saved if this needless layer were eliminated, I asked? Are those not two simple questions?

As surprising as it may seem, I didn't get much of a response from that thrust or others. Most of the TOMs totally ignored my notes. Sarcasm didn't work. Shaming them, as in "this is the only place" approach, didn't work. Sledgehammers wouldn't have worked either. I decided nothing would and left. I had had enough. So had they.

Homework assignment:

Tri riting a noot two yur bos loded wit mizpelings. Its funn. Noww hitt zend.

NO LONGER WORKING BUT STILL PICKING NITS

26

Pushing the Envelope While Staying on the Cusp

Don't get me wrong, despite a ton of bellyaching I had a great time, much of the time. I loved the action amid all the frustrations of dealing with, or working around, a handful of lousy managers, big-headed anchors and incompetents or slackers who were always looking for an argument. Every shop I was in had a core of solid pros, people who knew what they were doing and were usually a delight to be around.

But I'm also glad it's over. After retiring, I found it hard at first to figure out the Help Wanted ads on JournalismJobs.com, seeking applicants with the ability to work across all "platforms." It wasn't a political guru they wanted but a journalist. They didn't talk like that when I was in news. Other ads asked for proficiency in things I'd never heard of, one of them being Freehand. What do you do with the hand that isn't free? Isn't that how you get warts?

There seemed to be new impediments to getting hired. *Newsday* ran an ad on JournalismJobs.com one spring for an Internet Manager whose "daily responsibilities include publishing articles, photos, polls, audio/visual and interactive content to a database-driven Web site on deadline." The ad from the Long Island-based newspaper cautioned, "A successful candidate will have reliable transportation."

Naturally, I immediately got on the computer and dreamed up potential responses from *Newsday* to the transportationally-challenged who answered the ad.

Dear Ms. Willey,

Although you have an impressive resumé and turned in a truly remarkable writing audition, a 1996 Geo Tracker does not strike the managers of *Newsday* as 'reliable transportation.' Sorry.

Dear Mr. Kirsch,

The hiring process at *Newsday* is a genuine team operation. One of our parking lot attendants noticed that the New York State inspection sticker on your 2007 Corolla has expired, so we will not be offering you a job.

Dear Mr. Lorenz,

Thanks for the laugh. That was a very funny letter, yet we trust that in a more serious mood you would agree with our opinion that a 'brand new American Flyer sled' doesn't really qualify as reliable transportation. We see that your last job was in Nome, Alaska. Good luck.

Dear Mr. Iliff,

We are returning your job application. We suggest you re-read our ad, more thoroughly this time. Should you ever get rid of that nasty looking green Kia feel free to contact us again.

Dear G.A.,

That is indeed a fine looking 2005 Fat Boy FLSTFI in the picture you sent us, and we'll take your word that it 'purrs like a baby, rides like a marshmallow.' We appreciate your affection for motorcycles, but *Newsday* doesn't see how that 'passion,' as you describe it, along with fourteen years experience in parachute maintenance, qualifies you for a job here. In addition, to respond to the note attached to your resumé, we aren't interested in serializing your autobiography, 'Fat On Fat.'

A few ads you re-read three or four times because they are so arrogant and outrageous. Take this one on JournalismJobs.com several Septembers ago from the *Kokomo Tribune*.

"We're looking for someone who can push the envelope and turn out edgy and compelling pieces... If you're a trend spotter who stays on the cusp of what's hot, new and fun, we're looking for you. From design to feature packages, we're willing to try anything once, but you've got to have the drive to work hard and a love of the business. If you don't, we're sure the local burger joint has an opening."

If I had been the least bit interested, here's what I would have sent them:

To the Editors of the *Kokomo Tribune*:

I'm a Hoosier, been in the news business more than 45 years and wouldn't mind being back home in Indiana, but before I freshen my resumé and round up my best clips perhaps you would be kind enough to answer a few questions.

Let's start with envelope pushing. What does that mean? What do you push the envelope with? Your nose, fingers or, dare I ask, something else? Where are you pushing the envelope to? Is a stamped envelope better for pushing than an unstamped one? Can a pushed envelope be re-used for something important, say a grocery list?

Can you elaborate, please, on what you consider 'edgy and compelling pieces'? Are they angry, opinionated articles that upset readers so much they feel compelled to throw the newspaper against the wall and/or attack reporters on the street?

Have previous 'trend spotters' at the *Kokomo Tribune* ended up with nicknames? Was Spot one of them? How does trend-spotting differ from just plain old copying what most everyone else in the news business is doing?

Are there any scientific studies on how long the average Joe can stay on the cusp? Does staying on the cusp hurt? Is it loud up there? After you've been on the cusp a long time, do you go home at night and hear drilling noises in your head?

Are you really sure that you're 'willing to try anything once'? How about a revised obit section that features pictures of the deceased propped up in their coffins? Or a summer series on high school reunions that focuses on how many pounds each attendee has put on since graduation with snazzy graphics showing the total weight gained by the entire class?

Wouldn't it be 'hot, new and fun' to design a wedding announcement section that gives all the usual stats along with the names of everyone the bride and groom are known to have slept with or are widely believed to have slept with? Talk about 'edgy and compelling'!

Most important of all, what's the deal with putting down employees of 'the local burger joint'? While I'm sure there are some terrific benefits associated with working at the *Kokomo Tribune*, can your people reach over and grab a free Egg McMuffin and coffee anytime they want to? Isn't a lot of daily journalism—police blotter stuff, anniversary announcements—about as challenging as assembling a quarter pounder with cheese at Mickey D's? Here's hoping you will take the time to get down off your high cusp (slowly so you don't cut yourself on anything edgy) and address some of these questions or, as we call them these days, issues. As Elvis would say, 'thank you, thank you very much.'

The person who wrote that ad was an ass. If he or she is still employed, let's hope it's not in journalism.

Can You Have a "Protected Characteristic" and Not Know It?

There's so much I don't understand these days. Another ad on

JournalismJobs.com, this one from *The New York Times,* contained the normal boilerplate about The New York Times Company being an equal opportunity employer that doesn't discriminate "on the basis of race, color, religion, gender, sexual orientation, marital status, age, disability, national origin, citizenship" and then this wrinkle, "or any other protected characteristic." What's that? How do you go about securing a "protected characteristic"?

During my time in newsrooms, my prime characteristics were undoubtedly sarcasm and yelling. Is one or both of those now protected? Does this mean if I were a TOM today and someone who badly bungled a project said, "Well, I did the best I could," I wouldn't get in trouble with the human resources crowd when I snapped, "Yeah, well maybe that's the problem."

A while back Newsday.com advertised in JournalismJobs.com for a "Vertical Product Specialist." What's that? An elevator operator? When I read on, I decided not. "The Vertical Product Specialist," the ad said, "will be responsible for product planning and execution of new mobile and newsletter products for Newsday Interactive throughout the full product lifecycle." I wish I could write like that.

The successful applicant would also be expected to work "closely with cross-functional teams to ensure financial and customer satisfaction goals are met." I don't know about you, but I've had a life-time goal of wanting to rub shoulders with a "cross-functional" team. As I see it, this would be a group of people who were really good at their jobs but argued among themselves — cross as hell — all the time. The constant bickering on the job should cut down on after work drinking sessions and maybe save a marriage or two.

If I were in a newsroom today, I probably wouldn't get much done because I wouldn't be able to stop laughing at some of the new titles that have been dreamed up. A person I really like was promoted by a major network to the rank of ingest manager. According to the announcement, my friend and another fellow would "serve as the first points of contact for all feed, tape and disk ingest."

I've ingested a lot of things I shouldn't have — my biggest failings were large chocolate bars after a huge meal and a generous goblet of brandy after many serious beverages—but I've never indulged in the eating of tape or disks. I wonder what wine you serve with a 1997 tape of "Face The Nation."

You have to be careful how you say "ingest manager." If you overheard someone saying that, you might think they were calling him an in jest manager. Looking back on all the clowning I did as a manager, maybe my title should have been in jest manager rather than executive editor.

If you weren't listening closely, you could also possibly think my friend's new position was incest manager, a vital post at summer camp to make sure teenage cousins kept a proper distance.

The announcement said the ingest managers would "develop and implement a new workflow for the intake of material." Journalists don't have trouble collecting material. The tough part is deciding what to throw away, what not to use. As far as I know, there wasn't a second company memo naming two egest managers. I only know that "egest" is the opposite of "ingest" because I looked it up.

When you get a promotion and a new title, it's human nature to want to tell your family and friends and brag a little. My friend (let's call him Matthew) is smart, and I can't imagine him firing off emails and making phone calls letting people know that he was now an ingest manager. Maybe he told them he was promoted to collection agent. That should have resulted in less giggling and head-shaking than ingest manager.

Although this was all new to me, it turned out that Matthew's network was jumping on the bandwagon long after other networks had appointed ingest managers. A couple of friends who brought me up to speed on the new broadcast nomenclature ridiculed two other trendy titles—content producer and digital journalist. Has anyone in broadcasting ever met a content producer? And what is a digital journalist? Someone who can count to ten or has all his fingers and toes?

I'd like to think that some creative soul, temporarily trapped at one of the networks, is working on a screenplay titled "The Invasion of the Ingest Managers." If it gets made into a movie, Nicolas Cage should play Matthew.

27

Absurd Roules and Practices in Newsrooms

Most newsrooms have a few preposterous rules that baffle the staff and spark a steady flow of in-house grumbling. These rules usually live on long after the TOMs who thought they were a great idea have left—the organization, the news business and even this life.

When I started at CBS News, Radio, there was a restriction on how soon a piece of tape—even a very essential or dramatic one—could be re-used on a newscast. If the president of the United States said, "I am not a crook" you obviously used the tape right away but had to wait a few hours before you could put that same cut on another newscast. During that interval, you scripted the key quote and had to make do with a less powerful piece of tape.

Huh? Exactly. It seemed nutty then and in today's world of constant repeats seems even nuttier. As a copy editor, there were times when I had a tape room re-cut the operative sound bite of a big story (start it a little earlier or trim the end of it) and then went to a manager to get approval to play it in afternoon drive for the many listeners who hadn't heard it yet. I can't remember being told "no" but having to ask felt demeaning and very odd.

That rule was discarded during my time as a TOM at CBS Radio, and, as far as I know, no one had a stroke or had to double their pain medication because of the long overdue change. While I'm sure some of the staff welcomed the move, others probably thought I was all wet all the time and this was simply additional proof.

One of my employers decided somewhere along the way to use the term "U.S. citizen" instead of "American" in talking about people from the United States. This was presented as a way of not insulting those who might be Mexican or Peruvian. They were also Americans, the reasoning went. True, but I think most of the time if someone calls a person an American they mean he or she is from the United States. While Canadians are Americans too, when I stayed with a Canadian friend at a bed and breakfast in Austria the owners didn't consider both of us Americans. We were equals, but my friend was a Canadian. I was an American.

Under the silly American rule, editors (most of them anyway) were coerced into changing "American" references in copy to "U.S. citizen" with absolutely no evidence to support this assertion. The desk didn't get on the phone and track down a relative of the person involved and ask, "Is she a U.S. citizen?" If U.S. immigration officials followed the same citizenship rationale as this newsroom, millions of folks living here from other parts of the Americas would be overjoyed. Most editors went along with what the TOMs wanted. Guess who didn't? It was ridiculous and stupid and I refused to do it.

The "All The News That's Fit To Print" people have their own strange rules too. In early 2010, *The New York Times* published a story about eleven letters J.D. Salinger wrote to a commercial artist, and throughout the piece Salinger's best known novel, "The Catcher in the Rye," was called "Catcher in the Rye."

I sent an email and received a polite response within hours from an editor at *The Times* (on a Saturday no less), stating that it was the newspaper's policy to drop the "The" at the beginning of book titles. (I take it he was talking about books mentioned in news stories not in book reviews.) The editor said he personally thought the policy was "bizarre," had argued against it in the past and would do so again. *The Times*, he said, was inconsistent in implementing the rule, noting that the paper's obit on Salinger had the book as "The Catcher in the Rye," and that readers and publishers frequently complained when "The" was cut from book titles.

In the paper's *Book Review* the following Sunday, "The" was the first word in eight of the sixteen books on the fiction bestseller list. The number one seller was "The Help," described in capsule form as a book about "a young white woman and two black maids in 1960s Mississippi." If *The Times* did a news story that truncated the title to "Help," someone who knew nothing about the book might at first glance think it was the history of SOS or the EMS service.

Until *The New York Times* changes its style rules, I think writers, just for the hell of it, ought to see if they can come up with titles that force the paper's editors to keep their hands off the opening "The." I'm thinking of writing a book called "The The Stutterer."

"How Would Anyone Know That?"

When I was a teenager, my buddies and I loved playing "under the covers." Sitting at a table at one of our hangouts, we would flip through the selections on the juke box and take turns calling out a song title or a line from a song followed by the words "under the covers." There was nothing funnier. "Love me tender, love me long" under the covers, "you ain't nothin' but a hound dog" under the covers, "great balls of fire" under the covers, "once I had a secret love" under the covers.

More than half a century later, finding the lyrics to many songs unintelligible, I now occasionally entertain myself when the news is on by shouting, "How would anyone know that?" Try it. It makes you feel a little better after your intelligence has been insulted, yet again.

In the fall of 2006, *Newsday* carried a front page report on sex offenders living on Long Island, and a day later an anchor at WCBS Radio in New York said, "Thousands of Long Islanders are shocked to learn that sex offenders live among them."

Time to scream: "How would anyone know that?"

How could such a claim — "thousands...are shocked" — be verified? Had WCBS or another news organization talked to "thousands of Long Islanders" recently, even if simply to tell them one or two terrible things about sex offenders on Long Island and then ask, "Are you shocked?" Not likely. What was the basis of the WCBS Radio assertion? Nothing more, I suspect, than run away assumption, personal opinion and fast typing or ad-libbing.

(I don't mean to single out the staff of WCBS. We all stumble at times. Living where I did, I heard WCBS more often than any other station.)

There are newscasters and writers who forget that their likes and dislikes are not necessarily shared by all of their audience. Late one February a New York radio anchor said, "I know we were all hoping for no more snow." No one likes snow? How about all the skiers, the snowboarders, the owners of motels and restaurants that house and feed winter visitors, the ski lift operators and ski resort employees, the guys with pickups who make extra money plowing roads and parking lots? How about me?

During her first few outings on the CBS Evening News, Katie Courie liked to say "everyone was waiting for" or "everyone was talking about." Not too much of an exaggeration.

Scream time. "How would anyone know that?"

"Everyone?" That would include Charles Manson, Bernie Madoff and the older man who rides his bike around my town picking up bottles for recycling. He's part of the "everyone" classification, right? He sure is. I'll go talk to him this afternoon and get an update on his views.

Is there any news story in which the word "everyone" could legitimately be used? I doubt it, yet you hear financial reporters use it. "Everyone was expecting the unemployment figures for March to be...." What they mean is "most of the business people I know were expecting" such and such. "Most people" or "almost everyone" takes up more space and more time than the "everyone" shorthand, but I submit the longer versions are usually more accurate in news stories and easier to make a case for. "Everyone" is an advertising word, and if you hear it in a newscast, beware.

(Okay, okay, I know. "Everyone" is in the title of this book. My defense: (a) this is a book and not a news story and (b) would you have bought a copy of something called "Damn Nearly Everyone Needs an Editor, Although Hardly Anyone Will Admit It"?)

When I turn on the radio or TV the day after a shooting at a school or business, I'm likely to scream "bullshit" or make a loud noise accompanied by rapid mumbling. What you tend to hear is: "People in Milwaukee are trying to figure out why Jayson Lee Wappinger took two of his grandfather's hunting rifles to school yesterday and opened fire...." Since when did "people" take over the job of the police? Many people in Milwaukee and elsewhere are probably disturbed by what happened but saying they are trying to "figure out" what set Jayson Lee off is essentially meaningless. It strikes me as lazy journalism, something easy to say on the air when you don't really have anything to say. Formula pablum.

Another favorite word in these situations is "motive" as if the acts of a crazy person have a logical explanation.

I've gone all this way and never sprung "closure" on you. Whew. What a crock of shit that word is. It's another crutch to use as a peg for a piece when you have nothing new to report or don't know what to say. Silence isn't a virtue in broadcasting. It ought to be at times. The favorite line by correspondents that "folks here just want closure" is beyond dumb. Doesn't it usually take a long time — perhaps never — for people to adjust to the death of a loved one or loved ones? It certainly takes longer than the attention span of journalists. Reporters may keep yapping about "closure" because they want to get the hell out of wherever they are and get back home.

"Mood" is another baloney word, one used by anchors when chatting with reporters in the field. "Hey, Bob, I know you just got to Baghdad yesterday, but tell us what's the mood of the people there." Despite never having seen one myself, apparently all reporters travel with a Moodometer. It's a battery-operated contraption, I guess, which works instantly in any country regardless of whether you speak the language or venture more than eight feet beyond the safety and comfort of your hotel. I'm not entirely sure how a Moodometer collects data. Whether you hold it up in the air, stick it in the dirt or a large body of water, or shove it up the ass of a local or your own ass? In any case, reporters on their way to strange countries should be reminded to turn on the Moodometer the second they arrive. Otherwise they won't know what the hell to say when asked about the mood. (I would feel differently if the mood question were tossed at a reporter who had lived in the country for more than five years. That's seldom the case.)

If an on-scene reporter isn't quizzed about the mood then she probably will be asked, "Stephanie, what are the people there in Riyadh saying?" If Stephanie—like many Americans, including myself—has limited language skills, two accurate answers would be "Hello" and "Welcome to the Sheraton." Honest answers, yes, although not good ones to articulate on the air if you are fond of regular paychecks.

The reporter asked to respond to this inanity is probably putting in a seventeen-hour day (minimum), has only limited access to the city or country she is reporting from and may rely on a translator for most of her dealings with the locals, meaning their opinions are filtered before they get to her. Smart correspondents usually handle this question about "what are the people of Riyadh saying" with something along the lines of "Well, Terry, the Minister of Information has told us ..." (here they throw in some meaningless blah-blah and then completely rehash the report they gave only a minute ago.)

Scream time. ARGHHHHH!

Scott, Scott. I'll Be Damned If Your Name Ain't Scott.

One of the most annoying affectations of American newscasts to me is the constant references to the anchor's first name by reporters doing live shots.

"Well, Scott, brokers here on Wall Street say...."
"Scott, President Obama came to the Heartland today hoping to...."

Who talks like that? If you and I were chatting and you threw in a "Larry" every other sentence, it would be very tiresome after about the third one. I know my name. I don't have to hear it every thirty seconds.

I'm not picking on CBS News here, nor Scott Pelley who, I think, is an okay anchor, although he or his producer seems obsessed with running over and over old snippets of interviews he's done that add nothing to what we know about a story. All the commercial networks play the name game. Doesn't it remind you of a little kid trying to get attention? "MOMMY, MOMMY, MOMMY!"

In the summer of 2007, I heard a two-minute radio newscast by

ABC anchor Charles Gibson in which reporters in the field called him "Charlie" at least four times. Why do TV and radio news managers and producers embrace the unnatural and the artificial? Is it their view that we in the audience are so out of it we need constant reminders of the anchor's name? Or are anchors paid by the number of times they can coax reporters to call them by their first names? (This is one of several things my wife and I don't agree on. Irene thinks this name calling adds a "personal touch." All these years I've spent trying to make her smarter and so little progress it seems.)

In real life, friends sometimes playfully call friends by their last names. If one network instructed its correspondents to refer to the anchor by his last name on the air — "Well, Pelley, brokers here on Wall Street say" — I wonder if the other nets would quickly copy that. As irrational as that sounds, nothing would surprise me.

Live shots are the obsession of the TOMs of news, something akin to the Second Coming. The Scripture, according to them, says that having a reporter on live from the scene gives the news more immediacy, more "now," maybe even more of an "edge." (Whenever news executives spout off about wanting pieces with an "edge," that suggests to me instructions to go as close as possible or even beyond the boundary — the edge — between news and opinion, and, by God, since orders are orders good reporters do as they are told.)

Sure, a live picture of the Capitol or the White House plasters a majestic and powerful image onto the screen, but television is a medium where visual images compete against words and information for our attention. Many live reports are ad-libbed from notes and often lack, I've always thought, the precision and clarity that can be delivered in a well-written and well-produced piece on tape. Taping a TV piece increases the chances you can spot and eliminate any obvious visual distractions that make it difficult to focus on the information being conveyed. You can always do a second or third take when you are taping.

"The less seen, the more heard. The eye is the enemy of the ear in real drama. All the masters knew this," playwright Thornton Wilder is quoted as saying by Arthur Gelb in "City Room." The news TOMs don't buy this. Pictures count, words are extraneous.

During the last presidential campaign, the CBS Evening News insisted on putting reporters live on the air from Republican political rallies, at times while one of the candidates was clearly visible on the stage in the background. It was very distracting and made worse by the reporters imitating golf announcers, speaking softly so they wouldn't upset the people who had come to hear the candidate speak.

Yes, there are times—and this is television at its best—when the pictures are so gripping they are all that matter. That doesn't happen a lot, and we're talking here about everyday journalism. The next time you watch television news with another person stop and listen to what the two of you say during the broadcast.

"Why's he standing in the rain? It's pouring. Look at his hair."

"Check out that microphone. Why's it so blue? Reminds me of cotton candy."

"God, the guy's bald. Bald! I've been watching him for years and never knew that. I've got more hair on my fist than he has on his head."

"What the hell is that on his face? There. That weird black goo on his left cheek? You don't see it?"

"What was that last piece about?"

"Beats me. What WAS that on his cheek?"

Minor details such as facts and context don't have much of a chance in that environment. My own suspicion is that TV news chiefs are in love with live shots because the technology exists to do them, and when a reporter has little new to say pictures of any kind help disguise that reality. The perils of live, on-scene reporting were underscored for me by a WABC-TV Eye Witness News correspondent sent to stand outside the Dakota building in Manhattan the night in 1980 when John Lennon was shot. Although not a verbatim, this is in essence what the reporter said LIVE and ON-SCENE: "John Lennon dead. John Lennon shot to death. I can't believe it. John Lennon's dead. Shot. I can't believe it."

I was among those left wondering when in the hell the reporter would start believing it and try to find out some, uh, shall we say, facts.

When I was in the business, a serious drawback to live reports from journalists on the scene at a major breaking story was that they were on the air so much — with their network as well as with affiliates — they had no time to do any reporting themselves and probably knew less about the news they were "covering" than the guy in the FedEx truck making his rounds a hundred miles away. Often any new details the live reporter spewed out were whispered into his ear by a producer who was reading the latest lead from AP or Reuters or passing on an element from another reporter or producer working the story by phone and Internet. Welcome to the wonderful world of live journalism. With all the information now available on smartphones and other devices, on-site reporters have a much better chance of finding out for themselves what various sources are saying and what is on Twitter and the wire services.

I suppose the TOMs would argue that work with focus groups shows that viewers and listeners say they like a live presence where news is being made. With the push on these days to rely more on the contributions of citizen journalists, it may not be long before many full-time professional journalists are unemployed. If all news were gathered and presented by citizen journalists in a format approved by focus groups, it certainly would save network shareholders a ton of dough, including millions for satellites, makeup and hair spray. Would the product be any worse than it is sometimes these days? Maybe not.

28

it's Time for an Editor's Code of Conduct

$\mathcal{A}$ dispute a few years ago over the quality of a completed project reportedly led a veteran editor of *The Washington Post* to punch a reporter after the reporter called him a three-syllable word beginning with "c." Every account I've read indicates the word wasn't "cowpuncher."

That incident coming more than thirty years after I slugged a subordinate at Radio Free Europe shows me that newsrooms need an Editor's Code of Conduct. Here's a rough draft of what one might look like.

I (insert name) do hereby pledge that I will never slap, stab, slug, shoot, strangle, or suffocate a writer/reporter nor will I scream "you stupid son of a bitch" or "you're the biggest asshole I've ever met and you obviously come from a long line of assholes" when the previously mentioned person turns in copy, either near or far from deadline, in which:

(1) The lead sentence begins with the word "meanwhile."

(2) The lead sentence is eighty-seven words long, has nine commas, four parenthetical thoughts and ends with a question mark.

(3) Montana is described as a state in the Midwest.

(4) The writer/reporter, when questioned about a key element in the story, says, "How would I know? I don't understand it myself."

(5) A person named Miles Brewster IV is quoted as an eyewitness to a big apartment fire in Connecticut when three weeks earlier a Miles Brewster IV was said to be the only person who saw a mother drive her car and her kids into a lake in Utah.

(6) The name of the town from which the reporter is allegedly reporting is consistently misspelled.

(7) The lead paragraph says so-and-so was badly hurt in an accident, and the fact that this person is now the late so-and-so is buried in the eleventh paragraph.

(8) The expressions "as everyone knows" or "as is obvious to anyone" are used.

(9) The writer/reporter refuses to include any meaningful background information, claiming "we've already reported that."

(10) A radio talk show host is portrayed as speaking for "Middle America," wherever that is.

(11) The copy looks exactly like what was on the AP wire minutes ago, including the same six typos.

(12) An analysis piece ends with the wishy-washy "only time will tell."

(13) The writer/reporter misuses (after having the difference explained to him 2,367 times) the words "infer" or "imply."

(14) The writer/reporter, when asked about a quote that doesn't make sense, says, "Well, I think that's what she said. I didn't write that part down."

(15) Any politician who isn't from the East Coast or the West Coast is said to be "a leading representative of the Bible Belt."

(16) The winners of the World Series are called the "World Champions."

That's as far as I've got. An Editor's Code of Conduct probably would also need a line or two reminding signatories that there should be no uninvited touching of other staff members (either above or below the waist, either in the office or out), and a reiteration that baseball bats, blow torches and hedge trimmers are forbidden in the newsroom.

29

Five Ways to Improve the Modern Newsroom

 merican newsrooms have failed miserably in keeping their personnel policies up to speed with the spectacular advances in technology and the resulting changes in social behavior. Bad habits can quickly become the norm. Here are five simple steps to restore badly-needed discipline to the workplace.

1. NUNS WITH RULERS

Sisters from the Order of St. Jalapeno, the patron saint of the unfocused, roam the premises 24/7, ruler in hand; no plastic, junky ones, only wooden ones with that metal strip on the edge, so it really hurts. Why is this necessary? Because in many newsrooms, employees devote much of their time to texting on their smartphones, tweeting, private emails, vital Facebook postings about their lunch plans and how their day is going, Google searches of potential vacation spots, browsing You Tube, endless chatting about cable TV's unwavering devotion to the futile searches for missing white women in foreign countries and checking eBay every ten minutes for the latest price on a 1956 Rocky Colavito baseball card. A covey of very short, very spunky nuns with quick wrists could go a long way to putting a lid on this conduct. The nuns' salaries (or whatever accounting decided to label them) might be tax deductible.

2. SQUIRT GUNS

As a backup to the nuns, TOMS and a few designated editors would be armed with squirt guns and giant water bottles. If the whacking by the nuns of those who made or received a personal call or texted or tweeted while supposedly working on a story didn't do the trick, they would be considered free range chickens and their feathers soaked repeatedly with squirt guns until they stopped fiddling with their phones. Should they flee the immediate area, smartphone in hand, they would be vigorously pursued by the squirt gun SEALS. (Yes, it is possible that if this step is strictly enforced a few TOMs would be required to squirt themselves or each other. It's about time. Nothing's more wonderful than a good fight among the TOMs.)

3. ELECTRONIC ANKLE BRACELETS

These are needed because once people finish a long, personal email or a smartphone call, text or tweet they're exhausted and feel they deserve a break. After leaving their desk for a coffee or a granola bar, they wander off to the ladies or gents and then spend ten to fifteen minutes, minimum, standing outside the bathroom door talking about how much they might have in the bank now if they hadn't thrown away all those Rocky Colavito baseball cards way back when. A properly-run office, one with an ample supply of electronic ankle bracelets, would keep these malingerers in check, so they don't keep constantly wandering off when there is copy that needs to be edited.

4. DRESS CODE - NO FLIP FLOPS, NO SANDALS, NO SHORTS

This code, which also prohibits T-shirts and tank tops, would be in place every day of the year for obvious reasons. The banned items are casual wear intended for beach, bar or backyard barbecue where the intent is to crash and relax. Work isn't supposed to be relaxing or there wouldn't be a separate word for it, would there? Some newsrooms are so laid back on Fridays in the summer and on weekends all year round the only thing missing is a sign declaring, "Happy Hour — 10 a.m. To Whenever?" A newsroom shouldn't be confused with a cabana at Myrtle Beach.

5. FOOD CODE - NO FISH, NO CHEESE - NO EXCEPTIONS

Most newsrooms have a microwave and a refrigerator with lots of traffic to and from them. As long as slobs are clinically and legally classified as people, it will be illegal to shoot them for leaving the microwave and fridge areas a mess. Easier to enforce would be a blanket ban on fish of any kind at any time and cheese of any kind at any time. The smell from either or both can be overpowering, not to mention very upsetting to those trying to get some real work done, a category that normally includes one or two poor devils on every shift.

Although any or all of these changes would be very unpopular, I'm open to arguments on why they wouldn't force many hesitant journalists to become reacquainted with the tasks they are being paid to do.

30

The Lost Roundup

Though this may sound extremely conceited, among the reasons I'm delighted to be out of the copy editing business is the quality of the writing done by too many anchors these days. With enough time and warning, it is possible for a dedicated editor to make bad copy fairly decent.

The output of some anchors is beyond salvaging. Many of these characters resist almost all editing. A favorite stratagem is to claim that changes in their script amount to tampering with their style. Bullshit. Far too many editors give in rather than have a confrontation every hour on the hour. This means anchors head into studios with copy that isn't clear or is needlessly complex or—and this seems to be the new trend—so sparse it borders on gibberish.

A devotee of the less is best school, someone we shall call Don Miller, was the substitute anchor one winter morning in 2011 on "The CBS World News Roundup," the network's premier radio broadcast. I found the copy irritating and incoherent and emailed my thoughts to journalists at CBS and elsewhere:

> Don.
> Don Miller anchored this morning.
> Thursday.
> He.
> Don.
> Likes to start many stories with just a noun.
> Or a half sentence.
> 'No answer' was how the lead story began.
> Planes.
> Don talked about planes.

Planes at Reagan airport.

A CBS News Correspondent also talked about planes.

Ah.

What kind of planes?

Neither told us.

Ah.

The paper says they were passenger planes.

Takes too much time to tell us that.

'The latest on Libya' was how one story began.

In fact it was what happened last night.

That's the latest?

Libya segment also had reference to 'he.'

A CBS News analyst talked and talked about 'he.'

'He' was never named.

The guesses of who 'he' could be include Sarkozy, Gaddafi, and one supposes, Coco Laboy.

Don.

Miller.

Roundup.

#$%^&*(#$%^&*

31

Ned Smathers Tells How it's Done

It took me a long time to accept that there are people who don't think it's necessary to invest lots of energy and emotion at work, that there's no reason to try as hard as you can all the time. I still can't comprehend how talented men and women can be so lazy or lackadaisical while TOMs, for whatever reasons, look the other way. Careless, know-it-all anchors were the ones who really got under my skin. Hoping to make my point, here's an imaginary interview with one.

Vogel's Radio Digest thought it would be worthwhile to interview a top network radio anchor, so we sat down recently with Ned Smathers of NBF News. After many years at major market stations, Smathers now does afternoon drive for the NBF Network.

VRD: Tell us about your work habits, Ned. We often hear that reading in, that hour or more anchors spend looking at the wire services and websites before they begin writing their first cast of the day, is the most crucial part of an anchor's shift. Do you agree?

Smathers: Oh my, no. Absolutely not. Reading in is highly overrated. I already know what's going on when I get to work. If you wait until you plop down in front of a newsroom computer, it's hopeless. I think....

VRD: How do you know what's happening around the world if you don't look at the wires and websites?

Smathers: By listening to the radio and cable TV all day long. That way I already know the big stories before I step into the newsroom. Once I'm there, there's no need to fritter away my day by relying on the wires or websites for information. I already know the basics.

VRD: But don't stories change? Aren't there new details, new angles that are reported after you arrive?

Smathers: Occasionally. But I'm always on top of any late developments, either by spotting a scroll on one of the cable channels or sometimes a producer or another anchor will point something out to me.

VRD: So if you don't "fritter away" your day, as you put it, reading in, what do you do before you start writing?

Smathers: Pelvic tilts.

VRD: Pelvic tilts? You're putting me on.

Smathers: Am not. They're good for you. Good for the disks. Plus they help with my breathing when I'm on the air. An added bonus to doing pelvic tilts while sitting down is that the desk assistants, especially the young ladies, love to watch you do them. I would be lying if I didn't admit it's a real kick to be tilting when you know some of those little sweethearts are enjoying it so much. Maybe you shouldn't print that.

VRD: Some, make that many, of your newscasts sound as if you don't have a script, that you haven't written anything before you go into the studio. That's not possible is it at the network level?

Smathers: Thank you, thank you. That's a huge compliment. I want to sound as if I'm ad-libbing, that I'm giving the news in a conversational, spontaneous fashion. I really try to work on that part of my delivery. I do have a script, of sorts. Usually I write several stories the conventional way but at times—especially if my pelvic tilts are going well that day and I'm really relaxed—I'll scribble down notes on a couple of other stories before I hightail it into the studio.

VRD: In preparing for this interview, I listened to maybe a month's worth of your broadcasts, and one thing that really struck me is how often you never identify who's talking in a sound bite or a correspondent's report. One newscast had President Obama talking and you never identified him before or after the sound bite. I was....

Smathers: So?

VRD: Well, don't you think you should have, so people knew who was speaking, that it was the president?

Smathers: Obviously not. Just because he's president doesn't mean I have to fawn all over him and mention his name every time we use a sound bite of him. People who can't identify his voice aren't listening to my broadcasts anyway, and even if they were I see no need to insult the intelligence of other listeners by giving the president's name every damn time we provide him valuable air time to spread his, frankly, very twisted message.

VRD: Do your bosses know you talk like that off the air about the president?

Smathers: Don't know, don't care. I'm entitled to my opinions. Do you have other questions?

VRD: I'd like to pursue this not identifying voices on your news-casts, though I doubt it will get me anywhere. I heard one of your casts in which NBF's long-time Washington correspondent Ron Walsh was talking about Obama and what had happened in the lame-duck session of Congress, but Walsh was never identified before or after he spoke. Why?

Smathers: Why not?

VRD: Shouldn't a listener be told who is speaking and maybe some hint of why the speaker is qualified to be talking about the subject?

Smathers: Not necessarily. That's so old-fashioned. We've moved beyond that. We're trying to present the news and give folks the latest information. Who the speaker is, is ultimately unimportant. It's the information being imparted that counts. I say get the facts and informa-tion out there and don't clutter up things with a bunch of meaningless IDs that will be forgotten two minutes after the broadcast is over.

VRD: A week or so ago you did a story on Afghanistan and used a cut of someone who sounded like a reporter, but you never named the person. A friend who heard the broadcast with me knew the voice was that of NBF's Pentagon correspondent. Do reporters complain if you use a piece by them but never give their name?

Smathers: Listen to what you just asked — "Do reporters com-plain?" All reporters complain. It's the nature of the beast. I say ignore them. Let's face it, that's what most reporters do best, complain.

VRD: I assume NBF News has editors. Do they object when you hand them a script in which a correspondent isn't identified?

Smathers: They can object all they want. It doesn't matter. Some of them even try to fiddle with my script. I simply don't stand for that. That's not their job. The only thing they're there for is to make sure I have the best and latest sound bites and reports available. They're not being paid to fool with my writing style, which, if I do say so, has proven very popular for quite a long time now. Nor are they there to moan, as a few of these pipsqueaks do, about something they don't think is clear. If they focused a little more on the big picture — a smooth flowing newscast with good sound and different voices and a generous mix of stories — we'd all be better off. It's not my fault if they're so dense they can't understand something I've written. For God's sake, I'm not broadcasting to them. My obligation is to my national audience not these East Coast Rutgers' sissies.

VRD: A producer at another network whose judgment I respect pointed out that you have a habit of not immediately telling listeners where a story is taking place. This producer heard one of your casts in which the lead-in to a reporter's piece mentioned "West Coasters" and then the reporter talked about "the city," but what city was never named. Ever. The only clue came after the piece when you gave the call letters of the reporter's station. Isn't that....

Smathers: No. Whatever you were going to say the answer is "no." Your producer buddy is another do-gooder harping about minutiae. Listeners on the West Coast wouldn't need those meaningless details spelled out for them. Once again, it's the information that's paramount, not the reporter's name or some editor's silly fixation on, la de da, clarity. These clowns ought to look around. That's why newspapers are dying all over the place. People don't want long, dull stories loaded with too many facts and details.

VRD: Several of us at Vogel's Radio Digest have noticed that many times you are very casual about providing a source for a story. You'll say something like "a big counterfeit ring is broken up — 10 people who had been making phony 100 dollar bills from Maine to Maryland arrested." That's an allegation or a charge, yet you seldom make that clear until much later in your story. What do you say to those who think that's second-rate journalism?

Smathers: Let them audition for my job and see if they get it.

(Laughs.) Seriously, many anchors, including some at my own network, get bogged down in all kinds of sourcing at the start of an item. That really interrupts the rhythm of a story, so why do it? Anyone arrested in this country has probably done something bad or the cops wouldn't have brought them in. I've been at this a long time, and I know what I'm doing and how to do it. By the way, you look very uncomfortable. Are you okay?

VRD: Yes, I'm fine. Why do you ask?

Smathers: Well, you probably noticed I've been doing some pelvic tilts as we talked and that makes some people very, very uncomfortable. It's okay. You wouldn't be the first person who refused to admit they were uneasy when I was tilting. Anyway, go on.

VRD: There has been criticism of your newscasts — listeners send lots of notes to our website about you — that your broadcasts are a hodgepodge of strange, random noises and sounds that are frequently never explained. One listener who signed himself TL said most of your newscasts don't make sense. How do you respond to that criticism?

Smathers: Simple. Most of life doesn't make sense. Why should my newscasts?

VRD: I guess we stop there. Thank you, Ned, for spending time with us.

Smathers: Absolutely, my pleasure. Thanks for listening. You look awfully tense. Try some pelvic tilts.

32

Questions, Questions, Questions

*A*re you annoyed when you turn on a radio newscast and the anchor sounds as if he is trying to read copy and suck on a Life Saver at the same time? Good. I'm not alone then. There's an anchor on a commercial radio network who does this. I wonder why. Does he think it gives his voice a juicy, informal, inviting quality? Has no one ever told him this habit—or whatever it is—makes him unlistenable?

If you have a pulse, you probably have lots of questions about what you see and hear on TV and radio and on the Internet. Here are but a few of mine.

When someone at MSNBC.com writes a headline, is it edited by another person before it appears on the website? If so, is the editor who approved "Military Tightens Rules On Military Discharges," the same one who didn't spot a problem with "Whales Perform For First Time Since Death"? And could this same person have okayed a picture caption of Hugh Hefner, stating he was "still hard at work"? I think I know the answers. Editing is an increasingly unappreciated skill. Editors are seen as a luxury in a time of tight budgets, an unessential component that can be chopped from the head count. When editors are viewed as dinosaurs, the copy churned out by anchors and reporters sometimes seems to have been written by dinosaurs.

News organizations, big and small, have problems with head-lines. In 2005 my hometown paper, *The Times* of Frankfort, Indiana, told readers "Developer Pulls His Mulberry Project," which frankly sounds thoroughly enjoyable. In 2009 *Newsday*, the major Long Island paper, declared "Nut Recall Widens." And not a moment too soon.

But back to the questions. How many AP subscribers either asked for a refund or gave notice they were cancelling their contracts after the agency reported that Paul Harvey, a "talk show pioneer," had died? I don't think it would be going out on a limb to say with confidence that whoever wrote that had never heard a Harvey broadcast.

Why do anchors, especially those at Fox News, tell viewers "you won't believe this next story?" How do they know what any of us would or wouldn't believe?

Did the herd mentality in commercial broadcasting nag at the other TV networks when CBS News let Morgan Freeman drop the final "r" in "headquarters" in his introduction to Katie Couric's evening broadcast? Did the other nets consider doing the same? If Freeman could say Couric was reporting from CBS News "hed-quar-tuhs" were CBS News correspondents tempted to see if they could get away with skipping the last "r" in "quarters," "borders," "ranchers" and "daughters"?

Was that an exclusive by Agence France-Presse early in 2010 when it reported "hazardous roads killed two people" during a storm along the East Coast? Was there any explanation of how the roads did this? Any amateur video from cell phones? Do car insurance companies pay survivors' benefits when all of a sudden a road turns violent and starts killing people? Can killer roads be prosecuted?

Do you understand why the CBS News budget has apparently never been large enough to afford a comb for Lesley Stahl? Is it possible that even if she had a comb no one in authority would have ordered her to use it?

Why do anchors use up valuable air time (a) thanking correspondents for doing a report? Isn't that their job? And (b) with silly transitions—"turning to the Middle East," "back in this country," "turning now to news closer to home"?

When Fox News flashes a graphic on the screen saying "Fox Fact," what comes into your mind? Do you wonder if it's really a fact or only something those employed by Fox News believe to be true?

Is what Fox News does any more troublesome than what the CBS Evening News did one summer night in running a graphic that said "FACT" when quoting a White House statement that denied something North Korea had said? Is it the view of CBS News that everything said by the White House is a fact? Should anchors at CBS News, Radio be allowed, as one did in early 2012, to use the pronoun "we" when talking about the U.S. Government? Is CBS News now a wing of the U.S. Government? If so, am I the last to find this out?

Do reporters or stringers who predict the future get an extra fee for being a prognosticator? A few years back a reporter in Brazil told listeners in a very authoritative voice what the toughest problem a young boy in a custody case would face in the future. Not MIGHT face in the days and years ahead but WOULD face. Shouldn't reporters report and not predict?

Did anyone besides me tune into a CBS News special on the death of Ted Kennedy mainly to see what had happened to Katie Couric? In closing the evening news, Couric promoted a special on Senator Kennedy coming up at eight p.m. Eastern, saying "until then I'm Katie Couric." I couldn't wait for eight p.m. to roll around. When I turned the TV back on at eight, who would Katie be? Charles Osgood? Harry Smith? Kate Smith? Oprah? Jackie Gleason? Nope. Couric looked the same to me. She hadn't changed a bit. It's not the first time a broadcaster has disappointed me. Did such clumsy wording — "until then I'm Katie Couric" — grate on anyone at CBS News management?

Did any of the TOMs at CBS say a word to the anchor and editor after this pearl was heard on a CBS News Update about Congressman Anthony Weiner: "a senior New York Democrat says Weiner's hope is he can stick it out"? Weiner was already in deep trouble for sending pictures of himself to women who weren't his wife, and, unless he was a complete ignoramus, he probably knew it was not a good time to stick anything out.

When Sean McManus was president of CBS News, I sent him emails from time-to-time, usually pointing out things I thought CBS had done wrong or stories they should have skipped altogether. His responses tended to be brief. In fact, he responded only once and then in one word — "thanks" — when I praised an Evening News piece for being, in my opinion, very clever and well done.

Many times afternoon radio newscasts triggered the impulse to send an email to McManus. Here are two emails picked from a fairly sizeable collection:

November 9, 2010
Dear Mr. McManus,

You might like to listen to today's four p.m. radio newscast. There is a strong editorial tone to the lead, not a hard news tone.

There is a piece dealing with a review by the U.S. Government of the Afghan war and then someone talks. This someone — reporter, expert, politician — is never identified. There is a story about the cruise ship in trouble that begins with the words 'the Carnival's Splendor,' as though all listeners know what the anchor is talking about. In the second sentence of this story, the anchor gets around to mentioning that this is a 'ship.'

There is a story about some survey done (I think) by an outfit called BBO. What BBO is is never explained? Someone named Doug Hart talks about the survey, but listeners aren't told who Mr. Hart is.

Does CBS News no longer employ editors?

Sincerely,

Larry McCoy

December 29, 2010
Dear Mr. McManus,

At five p.m. Eastern time today the CBS News, Radio Hourly began with these words:
'Those who fight to stop Islamic terrorists chalk up a win, this time in Denmark.'

I gather that the five people arrested are guilty and there will be no trial. This seems to be a CBS News Exclusive.

Sincerely,

Larry McCoy

My thoughts about this particular anchor have also been shared on Facebook. Here's a posting from September 2013:

Whenever I sense my natural reservoir of sarcasm is running a tad low, I go to the Internet and listen to an afternoon newscast by an anchor at a major network. Listening to this person usually perks me up.... It's almost always hard to know what he is talking about, difficult to tell where one 'story' ends and another begins. This afternoon two medical pieces ran together as did a story about the 9/11 observations and an attack in the Sinai. I have a suggestion: why doesn't this network have a "desk associate" (née desk assistant) sit in the studio with the anchor and blow a whistle when one story ends and another begins?

After Scott Pelley became anchor of the CBS Evening News and Patricia Shevlin, the executive producer, I found myself spouting off a little less at the TV about some damnable thing that had just been on the air. When Couric was anchoring, there were many nights when Irene told me to put a lid on it and suggested I stop pestering McManus with emails. "They must think you're a crank." That's ludicrous. How could anyone possibly think that?

33

Rockin' Cooper — Tweet, Tweet, Tweet

Although I rarely watch cable news, when I do it's clear why around-the-clock television news may be the worst thing ever conceived. One November night in 2011, with the New York Knicks comfortably ahead of the Chicago Bulls, I switched over to CNN to see if anything was going on. You know—news from somewhere in the world, something of significance that might have an impact on my life or those of my kids and grandkids. Or something gripping, perhaps dramatic footage of flooding, a small child trapped in a well or a moving speech by someone.

Anderson Cooper was on, and he was just beginning a segment (or perhaps a figment) about Sarah Palin's Twitter page. Something that had been on the page was no longer there. Holy Mother of Sacred Frocks! Was my brother in Missouri aware of this? Should I tell him? How about my sister in Indiana? Is this something she needs to know right away? I've got a brother in California. Should I call him and simply scream, "Turn on CNN!" and then hang up?

I didn't get on the phone to anyone. I didn't even call upstairs to Irene. What I did was almost wet myself. I was frozen, could not move. I couldn't believe what I was hearing. The only thing that comes close to this paralysis was the time I and a couple of other Americans were in the office of a top gun at Radio Free Europe, complaining about how little money we took home after paying both U.S. and German Social Security and taxes, and he said if we didn't like it "you could always give up your passports." I have a very short fuse but didn't explode that day because I couldn't believe anyone would say that.

This time I couldn't believe anyone would say on television what Anderson Cooper was saying. Palin had changed something on her Twitter page! Read all about it! What are the long-range ramifications of this? Is there any sign of activity at the Pentagon? Should calls be made to Henry Kissinger and Zbigniew Brzezinski to get their assessments? What's Wall Street likely to think of this? Have the Asian markets reacted yet? Are the other nets gearing up for wall-to-wall coverage?

It seems all this excitement on CNN involved a tweet from the conservative writer and commentator Ann Coulter that had been put on Palin's Twitter page and listed among Palin's Favorites. Cooper kept calling what had appeared on the Palin page a retweet. (Question for linguists: if someone else had picked up the Palin page's retweet of the Coulter tweet would it be correct to describe this as (a) a triple tweet, (b) a tweet, tweet, tweet, (c) a three tweet or (d) malarkey?)

The Coulter tweet concerned a sign outside the Harlem church of a habitual critic of President Barack Obama, accusing him of being a Taliban Muslim and an "illegally elected president." As I said, this tweet was picked up by the Palin Twitter page and ranked in its Favorites list, but now it had been removed. In other words, the Palin Twitter page had done a retreat from the retweet. Cooper interviewed a young man who said that he and Coulter, despite very different views on most things, frequently exchanged tweets about this African-American minister and his harangues against President Obama.

Admittedly this was frightening stuff—"Good God, Helen. Now's not the time to argue. Get the kids and get in the cellar!"—but political sluggard that I am I went back to the Knicks´ game. During a time out, I looked in on CNN again and the saga of the disappearing retweet was still in full bloom.

When I mentioned this tweet, retweet business to two working television journalists, they immediately made the point that you have to fill the time and that can be awfully difficult some days. True, but wasn't there anything else CNN could have done to burn up ten minutes or more? A feature? A repeat of a hard news story? Even re-runs of the video showing Wolf Blitzer on a camel would have been better.

The allegations on the church sign were offensive, I believe, and Palin could be criticized for giving them wider circulation before they were taken off her Twitter page. But after Palin left her job as governor of Alaska before her term was up was anything she did or didn't do a surprise? I couldn't be the only voter in 2011 who wasn't interested in every breath and gesture of Palin and other potential 2012 presidential candidates. We were even less interested in analysis of those breaths and gestures.

The attention given to the Harlem church sign underscored for me how our technology is far ahead of our common sense. It is now possible for the opinions, distortions, or lies of millions of folks around the globe—halfwits and know-nothings included—to be instantly disseminated. But just because we have the capability to do it, doesn't mean we should, does it? When a wildly intemperate statement pops up on Twitter or on a video feed, should it automatically warrant wider exposure or are there still editors and producers who insist on checking if the speaker is someone with a genuine following or represents only himself and fifteen other people who flunked out of drum major school?

Should Anderson Cooper get swept up again in another tweet, retweet segment, we can only hope he livens it up with a little music. "Rockin' Robin," a hit by Bobby Day in the late '50s written by Leon René, would fit perfectly.

> "He rocks in the tree tops all day long
> "Hoppin' and a-boppin' and a-singin' his song.
> "All the little birds on J-Bird Street,
> "Love to hear the robin go tweet, tweet, tweet."

34

A Survey from T, The New York Times Style Magazine

One reason I consider myself lucky to have ended up in journalism is that I didn't have to dress up much. For years I wore blue jeans to the office, either with a shirt and tie or with a sweater. My interest in clothes is limited to the basics: is what I have on clean, is it comfortable and am I going to be warm enough or cool enough. To my mind, newspaper space and air time are too precious to squander on something as silly as fashion.

This makes me a huge fan of *T Magazine*, a thick, glossy thing that comes with the Sunday *New York Times* every few weeks. A colossal misuse of paper and ink, it is packed with smug articles and pictures of smug, glassy-eyed people, wearing expensive dust rags. Could it be that I invested time in dreaming up a fake survey after reading a real issue of *T*? Absolutely.

Dear *New York Times* Subscriber and *T Magazine* Reader,

Thanks for agreeing to complete this short survey about our exciting Men's Fall Fashion 2010 issue of *T Magazine*. We realize your time is valuable and appreciate your willingness to help the staff of *T* better satisfy your craving for bold, breathtaking statements in fashion and accessories.

Did you see the Calvin Klein ad in the front part of the latest *T*, the one where the model has his back to the camera and his pants lowered so the crack of his butt is visible?

Yes
No

If you answered yes, would you like to see more cracks in *T*?

Yes

No

Only if the models belong to the Tea Party.

The ad for jcrew.com showed a model sitting on a ladder in a suit and dress shoes but no socks. Does wearing a suit while going sockless strike you as:

Sexy and a real come-on.

Ridiculous.

No opinion or one I don't want to share with you.

In the Moncler clothing ad, there is a photograph of a man in an armchair reading a newspaper with a woman standing behind him while a large camel has his head and neck stretched out over both of them. Do you find it difficult to concentrate on your newspaper if there is a camel in the room with you?

Yes

No

If you answered yes, which of the following animals would you be more comfortable with in the room while trying to catch up on the news?

Tiger

Bambi

House-broken sperm whale

Dead barracuda

Wet walrus

The ad for Crate&Barrel shows a sofa on one page and on the

facing page a male model in cutoff shorts, above the ankle boots (and no visible socks), a dress shirt worn outside his pants, a shoulder bag and a pair of sunglasses in his hands. What was your first thought when you saw this model?

> I wouldn't get on a sofa with him.
> If he can't afford socks, he can't afford that sofa.
> I went totally blank for about ten minutes.

Would you be more inclined to buy something from Crate&Barrel if they learned how to space their name better?

> Yes
> No

In future issues of *T*, would you like to see more models whose sex, if any, isn't immediately apparent?

> Yes
> No
> Hell, why not ? Everything else is hard to figure out these days.

Did you see the short feature on clogs?

> Yes
> No

If you answered yes, what's your view on the assertion in the headline that "men's clogs are coming out of the kitchen this season"?

> Like hell they are. NIMBY.
> That does it. I'm going to stay in the kitchen.
> It's about time. They're so relaxing and they're good for your feet and back.

We ought to outlaw those damn things. This isn't Holland.

In reading the feature on clogs, were you surprised that there was some editorial content in *T* and not just a ton of wacky ads with wacky models who don't look like anyone you've ever seen on the street?

You betcha.
No
You call that content?

Were you shocked to see that a store you had actually heard of, Macy's, bought an ad in the fall issue of *T*?

Yes
No
"Shocked" doesn't even come close to describing my reaction. I was f---ing flabbergasted.

The full-page ad for 2xist Sliq has two men facing each other with nothing on but briefs, one with his arms folded, the other with his left hand behind his neck and his right hand pulling down the side of his underwear. What do you think the ad agency wanted you to think about the two models?

They were about to share a bucket of buffalo wings.
After the picture was taken, they swapped stories about scary airplane rides.
Whatever happens, happens and is no one else's business.
Those briefs look way too tight for the average guy.
How do you pronounce the name of the company selling this stuff?

An editorial feature called Manly Things quotes the "head men's-wear designer" of J.Crew Men's Shop as saying of an

Estwing hammer, "The more you use it, the more beautiful it becomes." Do you believe:

> He was talking about a hammer.
> He was talking about a body part.
> He is obviously working too many hours.
> He would have been more convincing if his left thumb, with a badly banged up fingernail, was partially visible.

In the six-page feature on leisure suits, half the models dressed in jackets and slacks aren't wearing shirts or even T-shirts. What was your reaction when you saw the bare-chested models?

> Why couldn't they have been women?
> When that style catches on big time, I'm moving to Iceland.
> That's one way to save money on ties.
> Why couldn't they have been women?

Would you like to see even more ads in the next issue of *T*?

> Yes
> No
> Don't think that's possible.

After looking at this or any other issue of *T*, which of the following sums up your overall impression of the magazine?:

> I'm glad I never go any place where people look so depressed and down-and-out.
> Something's messed up real bad if *The Times* won't print comics, but it prints this nonsense.
> Doesn't anyone sell combs anymore in this country?
> Anything as thick as *T Magazine* is obviously financed by the timber industry.
> I can't wait for the next issue.

This whole thing, the magazine and the survey, is a joke, right?

You're finished. Thanks for completing our 'I' survey. As a gesture of our gratitude for your time and input, we will soon email you a five dollar coupon for the latest book by our business editors, "Getting Inside Rupert Murdoch's Head and What We Found or Didn't Find There."

"Elitist Swill"

About a year later, after the dismal experience of thumbing through several other editions of *T Magazine*, I couldn't stop myself from composing a letter to the *Times's* TOMs.

August 24, 2011
Arthur Ochs Sulzberger Jr., Publisher
Bill Keller, Executive Editor
Sally Singer, Editor, *T*
Yasmin Namini, Senior V.P. Marketing and Circulation
Arthur S. Brisbane, Public Editor

Dear People of *The New York Times*,

Could we work out some type of arrangement where you would never deliver another copy of *T* to my house? Please! Last Saturday, *T* and several other elements of the Sunday edition were thrown on my lawn along with the Saturday paper. After a storm knocked out our TV satellite reception on Sunday evening, I decided, despite knowing better, to look at *T*.

The pictures on the contributors page included one of Didier Malige who was described as 'the hair visionary.' Malige's contribution was six full pages of girls with boys' haircuts. I don't know what it is you folks on Eighth Avenue find attractive and inviting, but back in Indiana, where I grew up, and out here on Long Island, where I now live, we know what boys look like and we don't want girls looking like boys. What the hell is wrong with you people?

Girls are wonderful. They're great to look at and fun to be with and talk to. Leave them alone. There are already enough boys. We don't need a bunch of girls conned into looking like fake boys. Okay?

Since Malige was described as 'the hair visionary,' I'm hoping that means he is one of a kind — the world's only 'hair visionary.' One is surely enough. But why do I think you probably have other 'visionaries' waiting in the wings to be introduced to your readers? Is there a nail visionary? If so, finger or toe or both? A leg visionary? Yes? No? An upper body visionary unknown and certainly unappreciated by ruffians like me?

It isn't only the odd people wearing very ugly clothes in unnatural poses that I find mindless. It's the copy too. The headline on one piece referred to a 'fantasy world of hardscrabble glamour.' I glanced at the article and could see no evidence the writer had tracked down a person who had a genuine hardscrabble existence and asked how big a part fantasies were in her life.

I implore you to spare me this elitist swill. Since I always stop home delivery when we're away, is it possible to get a schedule of *T* publication dates? That way I could synchronize my vacation plans with those dates and make sure I'm gone.

Or would it be easier for everyone involved if the circulation department simply informed the delivery company it was welcome to keep any and all of my copies of *T*?

I enjoy much of what is in the newspaper most days and hope we can find a mutually satisfactory and quick solution to this matter. One other point: if you insist on continuing this wretched *T* thing — and I'm sure you do — can't you at least find a few models who look as if they have enjoyed a couple of Big Macs or a plate of good old mac and cheese once in a while? Think about it! Please!

Sincerely,
Larry McCoy

Being pretty sure this is yet another instance where I'm out of step with today's news business, I didn't bother sending the letter to *The Times*. I did post it on my website, larrymccoyonline.com, and received several messages of support, which is always nice. But that damn magazine is still tossed on my yard several times a year. I'd leave it there if I weren't afraid it would kill the grass.

35

Don't Believe Everything You Read in the Papers, Especially Obits

If you've picked the right place to live, you don't have to die, at least not in your newspaper obituary. Had I never left Indiana, my obit in *The Indianapolis Star* might say that, despite all evidence to the contrary, "Larry McCoy went to be with his Lord" or that McCoy "passed into his Heavenly Father's Kingdom." In the summer of 2013, *The Times* of Frankfort, Indiana, my hometown, succinctly reported that a man "got his wings on Saturday."

Beyond the hyperbole about someone earning his eternal reward, obituaries and death notices can bear little resemblance to reality in other ways. Following the deaths of two people I knew well, the accounts of their lives in major newspapers contained preposterous claims about their talents, accomplishments and influence in journalism.

I don't think it's speaking ill of the dead to object when an obituary is so overblown that even the subject of the piece would cringe. In my dealings with these two individuals, I found them both to be competent journalists when not distracted by their vices, which was all too often.

It's a challenge to know what to say about those you spent many hours side-by-side with, but who were, in your view, troubled and, worst of all, couldn't always be counted on to meet deadlines. The trick is to find a clever way to say something that is civil and respectful but also accurate.

With that in mind, I offer the following suggestions on what you can truthfully say if asked about a dead person who wasn't exactly a giant in the profession:

"When Bill was on his game, there was no one better." (Real meaning: Bill was never on his game.)

"Sharon was the easiest person in the world to work with." (Real meaning: she was a zero and knew it, so she stayed out of your way.)

"Always worked very hard." (Real meaning: too bad he was always spinning his wheels.)

"We'll all miss Paul." (Real meaning: for a week. Maybe.)

"She was very dedicated and very determined." (Real meaning: dedicated to self-promotion and sucking up to all the bosses.)

"Ralph always had a smile and never got flustered." (Real meaning: he didn't have a clue.)

"A joy to be around." (Real meaning: if you have a soft spot for imbeciles.)

"Lenny always welcomed new staff members and was very helpful to them." (Real meaning: Lenny was aware if the new folks stayed for more than six months he would be taking orders from them.)

"Barbara was one of a kind." (Real meaning: thank heavens.)

"That's such sad news about Norman. He was so, so young." (Real meaning: and so unbelievably immature.)

"It was a privilege to have worked with Katherine. She was incredibly talented and her job was her life." (Real meaning: how sad is that?)

"No one ever said a bad word about Janet." (Real meaning: she was so hopeless why bother?)

"Everyone liked Matt." (Real meaning: especially when you looked at the schedule and saw he wasn't on your shift.)

"One of the most unusual persons I've ever met." (Real meaning: a complete loser.)

When my time comes, I'm hoping anyone who might have liked being around me in a newsroom won't use any of the lines above and will come up with something a little more flowery than "I'd rather not comment. There are children present."

36

The Gems in—and the Many Uses of—a Newspaper

*W*hen you're away from home, reading a local newspaper is an excellent way to discover what you're missing by not living there. Squirrel paprikash, for example. There was a recipe for that in a paper in the Catskill Mountains of New York, where hunting is a big deal. In addition to the squirrel paprikash recipe, there was one for carrot pie. That one I saved, the other one I didn't. My mother fixed squirrel that my dad had shot and skinned, and yes, she told us it was chicken. I loved my mother, but no, squirrel doesn't come close to tasting like chicken. It doesn't matter how much paprika or what else you smother it in, it still tastes like Uncle Brian's shoes.

There are small-town weeklies that print the entire police blotter, packed with traffic accidents and arrests for driving under the influence of something stronger than Dunkin' Donuts decaf. A weekly police report published in a Nashville, Indiana, newspaper listed calls by people who reported hearing noises or seeing strange cars in their neighborhoods. A few folks dialed 911 and, when an officer answered, said never mind, just testing my new phone. The cops must love those calls.

A visitor reading the police blotter in *The Herald,* a weekly in my part of Long Island, might be surprised by the number of young people, both male and female, arrested for peeing in public. My town is not devoid of bushes and being picked up for doing private business in public strikes me as sheer laziness. Can't a GPS system be programmed to find the closest tall bush?

Sometimes you learn new words in out-of-town newspapers. I didn't know what a "racino" was until I bought a copy of *The Portland Press Herald* in Maine. It's a race track with slot machines.

There's also humor to be found in small papers. In October of 2010, the lead article in an issue of *Dan's Papers*, a free newspaper run for years by Dan Rattiner on the East End of Long Island, dealt with the expense of collecting leaves. The article, written by Rattiner, recounted a meeting of the East Hampton Town Board on the leaf problem. According to the paper, uniformed leaf counters, using "handheld calculators," had determined that "last year's leaf total was 6,203,811,412,701."

A "Professor Angelo Levy" told the board meeting that he was "working on a serum which could be injected into trees to enable them to divest themselves of their leaves all on the same day." You don't find copy like that in *The New York Times* or *Newsday*, the papers I normally read. Rattiner's funny piece took some shots at the East Hampton supervisor who had apparently scuttled the previous leaf collection program. Like any smart political body, the East Hampton Town Board decided to delay, for at least a week, a decision on what to do about leaf pickup, or so Rattiner said.

Although classified ads barely exist these days in many major newspapers, they are still going strong in smaller publications and shouldn't be ignored as a source of amusement. This is from the Help Wanted section of the September 10, 2010 edition of Vermont's *Bennington Banner*:

PRINTING/PUBLISHING
OFFICE MANAGER

Busy office with many
Business units, must know
Quickbooks, Excel
and understand cost and
financial accounting for
various business
units/people, wear many
hats, must be able to
multi-task and have great

phone/customer service
skills, please send cover
letter and resume and
wage requirements
FREE toaster after 3
months!
Cambridge Pacific
891 State Road 22
PO Box 159
Cambridge, NY 12816
518.677.5988 8066 fax
info@pacific.com
cpacific.com

When I read the ad to Irene, she, as usual, had a good question, "What happens if you leave after three months and a day? Do you have to give the toaster back?"

I say again, it's good to be reminded that the world you live in is not the only one there is. Ads do that for me. Frankly, I find searching for an amusing morsel in the classified ads of a small-town paper more rewarding at times than the futility of trying to finish the crossword puzzle in *The New York Times* along about Thursday or Friday when the puzzles are harder.

Batter Up!

In the desperate fight to keep their print editions alive, newspaper publishers have completely ignored a major selling point: once you've read the latest news from Iran to Indiana your paper has many practical uses besides wrapping coffee grounds and potato peelings. These possibilities are particularly appealing to those of us who don't intend to spend the rest of our lives with heads bowed in fervent worship of an iPad, iPhone or BlackBerry.

A real newspaper—the kind you can touch and feel—is one gigantic scratchpad. All those white spaces inviting you to write lists and notes. What to tell the doctor about the pain in your right hip. What to buy at the supermarket, including the brand of olive oil you've been ordered never to get again. What to pack for an upcoming trip. What you saw the new hire doing today that the boss ought to know about ASAP.

There's always plenty of room in a margin or in the blank space of a big ad to jot down ideas for an overdue letter to a good friend who doesn't have a computer, or a reminder that the Volkswagen is due for its annual inspection by the end of the month or the title of a song you heard an hour ago and don't want to forget.

I scribble in my *New York Times* nearly every morning at breakfast. While I'm reading *The Times*, Irene has *Newsday* in front of her, trying to do Jumble, the scrambled word puzzle. When she gets stuck, I jot down in my *Times* the letters she couldn't figure out and try my luck at them. After a visit to the doctor or dentist, I always scrawl the date and time for my next visit on my handy newspaper, saving the assistant from wasting one of those little appointment cards. Before I retired, part of my routine was reading newspapers on the way to work and scratching notes on them (it helps if you have small handwriting) about stories, quotes or angles I thought we ought to be pursuing.

An old-fashioned newspaper can also be an important tool for personal security. After being mugged several years ago, I never walk to or from my car in a dark parking lot without a newspaper rolled into a tight spiral and firmly gripped in my right hand. A broadsheet may not be as broad as it once was, but if you roll it properly you have a fairly respectable weapon. The night I was attacked my newspapers were in my briefcase. Some good they did me there. (FYI, the muggers were two young men I'd never seen before, not—as you might have suspected—two guys I had insulted and belittled in a newsroom. Of course, there's always the chance the muggers were hired by someone I offended.)

A thick newspaper, when correctly utilized, can teach grandkids the value of improvisation. On a summer outing with my two oldest grandchildren, Nicholas and Rachel Parish, they asked if we could play baseball. After rummaging through the car trunk, we found a dirty tennis ball but no bat. Not a problem. Grandpa took his paper, rolled it length-wise as tight as he could, and voilà—we had a Louisville Slugger. The three of us took turns batting with it. At the time I owned a Gateway laptop and read a lot of news on it, but it would have been a poor substitute that day for my *New York Times*.

Newspapers have a long tradition, at least in my family, of being used to line cabinet drawers and the flooring under sinks. In the summer, they are employed as weapons to swat moths and flies. Try doing that with a Kindle or a laptop.

If publishers are smart, they will get together and put out an ebook, maybe call it "1,001 Ways to Re-Use Your Newspaper." They need to do something fast before all of us diehards who want a newspaper we can touch, feel, scribble on and use as a baseball bat are no longer around.

37

Sticking to My Guns About Fussing over Royals

One fall night in 2010 I found myself, once again, swearing at the TV. "The CBS Evening News with Katie Couric" was leading with the plans of Prince Wincelot to marry whatever-her-name-is. I switched to Brian Williams on NBC. More swearing. By me, not Brian. NBC's Knightly News was also leading with the Prince and Little Miss Twinkleface.

This was idiocy, total twaddle, I kept carping, in between cuss words. In the background, a voice, Irene's, was saying "people are interested in the royal family." What does she know? I was a journalist for 45 years. She worked for a publisher. Why doesn't she mind her own business?

There was only one hope left, "ABC's World News with Diane Sawyer." Hooray! They led with China. But wait, Sawyer was in Shanghai and that explains their choice. When she threw it to George Stephanopoulos, the first words out of his mouth were royal nonsense.

Someone—I know it was Dirty Harry but it should have been Donald Trump—once said "a man's got to know his limitations," and I certainly know two of mine as seen through the eyes of the Fluffsters who took over CBS News, Radio: the British royal family and winter snow storms were both non-stories in my book. The fact that millions of Americans seem obsessed with both didn't cut it with me.

All these years after Princess Diana, Prince Wincelot's mother, was killed in a car crash in Paris, I haven't changed my thoughts on the foolishness and stupidity of American media squandering their time and space on endless blather about clueless Brits who do little but ride from town to town waving and having their pictures taken. Big damn deal. Folks still active in the news business tell me they are appalled when their shops go berserk on royal coverage, but a job is a job so they keep their heads down, do what the TOMs ask and hope for a real story to come along.

I was also out of sync in my long-held view that "it snows in the winter," and, unless there was a major disruption of transport and commerce, it wasn't anything to get excited about. Newscasts shouldn't lead hour after hour with snow in the Midwest or wherever. Here too my views seemed to be shared by approximately nine other people in the United States, four of whom were deceased.

A man in his 70s is expected to be a little more mellow than when he was younger, and I'm willing to concede, ever so reluctantly, that I was wrong in regard to the interest in and impact of winter storms. Global warming may have contributed to a surge of bad weather. It would be refreshing though if reporters and producers could come up with slightly more original ways of covering winter storms besides sounds of shovels and snow blowers, video of stalled cars, people skiing on city streets and interviews with folks who say they're ready for spring.

My opinion about the royals of the United Kingdom, however, remains unshakeable. They will become newsworthy when they get off their asses and do something useful and worth remembering. Newscasts and newspapers aren't the place for fairy tales and daydreams about Prince Wincelot, his father, the Prince of Nails, and the rest of that bunch.

An organization with a catchy name needs to be formed to oppose fanatical overexposure to royalty. Whilst trying to reach a decision on what to call this group, here are some of the possibilities I considered:

MRS – More Royal Silliness
The Royal WC Society – (WC for Who Cares not Water Closet)
Y-CBS – You Can't Be Serious
ITS-MI – Isn't There Something More Important
RRR – Real Royal Rubbish (Said in a growling tone)
INIST – I'm Not Interested – So There
O-SHUTUP – Obviously Sauced Hucksters Up To Usual Prattle
WDC – We Don't Care
IN-VORT – I'm Not Viewing Or Reading This
WGARS – Who Gives A Royal S---

Shortly after posting this on my website, I got several suggestions, including:

HRH – Huge Ratings Hype
WTTBO – We Threw Those Bums Out

One reader declared, "Earth is a sitcom on Martian TV. British Royalty, the Knicks and Lady Gaga are some plot twists the long-running series producers inject to maintain viewer interest."

Another argued that there was in fact no prince and no upcoming wedding, that all the hoopla was a conspiracy to change the subject by members of a secret society, WASP, War Against Sarah Palin.

Looking at the WASP suggestion helped me decide on a name, WART — War Against Royal Twits. They truly are twits. As for Palin, I suspect you know what I think.

38

What I Wanted to Say to Garrison Keillor but Didn't

Walking to the New York subway one November night with one of our granddaughters, we passed Carnegie Hall, and I stopped and bent down to tell Daniella what a famous place it was and how talented musicians went there to play. Irene amplified my comments and then nudged me.

"I think that's Garrison Keillor ahead of us."

"Nah," I said. "He looks too thin."

"I'm sure it's Keillor. He's wearing red sneakers."

"I don't think so."

"Mr. Keillor?" Irene called, raising her voice a little.

Garrison Keillor turned around. Up close the star of "A Prairie Home Companion" looks like a gangly mathematics professor. Irene said, "We're from Indiana, and we really enjoy your show." After shaking our hands, Keillor turned his palms skyward and, apparently thinking we were tourists, asked, "Are you finding everything you want?"

"We live on Long Island," I said.

"Oh."

I asked, "You're not going to write for The New Yorker anymore?"

"Nah," dismissing the notion with a wave of his hand as he headed across the street.

Chalk one up for Irene's good eyes and instincts. I figure anytime you see a well-known person whose work you like you ought to say "hello," provided you do it quickly without being intrusive. You may never get another chance.

I once saw Jerry Reed standing by a water cooler in the CBS newsroom, so I hurried over and mumbled, "I like your songs."

"Thank you, Brother," Reed said, extending his hand.

Another time Robert Gates was in the newsroom. He was a private citizen then—before his days as defense secretary but after his term as CIA chief and long after he was a student at Indiana University. Larry McCoy, a graduate of Indiana University, who was employed by RFE when it was funded by the CIA, had a story about the CIA and I.U. that Gates absolutely had to hear. I introduced myself and my I.U. connection, and Gates said his daughter was a student there. Ah, that means he's going to like this story even better, and I began.

A young man I knew at RFE graduated from I. U. and was given a lie detector test when he applied for a post at the CIA. The test conductor had also attended I.U., and whenever he noticed someone had gone there he waited until the end of the test to ask a phony question about Nick's, a bar approximately 78 steps from what was once the university library.

"Have you ever been drunk at Nick's?" the test conductor asked.

"Well, it depends on what you mean by drunk," my friend replied.

Nothing but silence from Gates and the smallest of smiles. I was hoping for a laugh. I retreated to my office.

Years later when Irene saw a tall man in a suit and red sneakers on the streets of Manhattan I had no killer anecdote ready for Garrison Keillor either. But I wish I had told him that Irene and I and two close friends were at a live broadcast of his radio show at Town Hall in Manhattan two years earlier, and it was one of the best performances I've ever seen.

I was amazed by how well and how tightly produced the broadcast was. All that music, all those skits—no flubs, everything perfectly timed. And probably most impressive of all, when Keillor came out to do "The News from Lake Wobegon" I don't recall any notes in his hands, didn't see a prompter. He simply talked. Started a story, wandered off track a little, came back, may have wandered off again and somehow it all was connected. A perfect circle. Excellent.

I wanted to tell him how good Irene and I think the musicians are, and how fond we are of the talents of Fred Newman, "Mr. Fred Newman," as he is always called, the sound effects man. How sometimes we can't stop laughing when Keillor is reading a script, and Newman has to come up with the sounds of a rare animal or an unusual household gadget.

I wanted to tell him about long Saturday afternoon rides back to Long Island with my grandson after skiing in the Catskills. Many a time at six p.m. I have ejected a tape cassette or CD and turned on "A Prairie Home Companion." Nick never seemed intrigued by detective Guy Noir or other bits, but on one ride home several years ago Keillor and Newman were doing one of those wonderful fast-paced pieces with sound effects and Nick was laughing harder than I was. It was funny, clean and very well done. Radio these days isn't exactly jam-packed with that sort of material, is it?

Nick is in his mid-twenties, speaks three languages, knows much more about all sorts of things than I ever will and is certainly more mature than I was at his age, but I feel sorry for him. While his generation has iPhones, iPods and iTunes, it has no iDea — no idea how gripping radio is when it stimulates your imagination.

Nick never heard Wally Phillips talking on the radio in Chicago, cleverly weaving his voice in between bits of sound. Wally created an entire world of his own for a listener. He would say something, a voice would answer followed by the sound of a door suddenly opening. Wally would say something else and another voice would respond with a funny comment and then boom, music. It was a mile a minute, inventive and entertaining.

Nick never got to listen to Jean Shepherd tell a story, one story, on WOR in New York that took almost an hour. No actors helping him. Jean alone, in front of a microphone, talking. He never had the pleasure of hearing Dan Ingram doing an amusing, verbal scat over the opening bars of a record. These weren't just isolated pockets of good radio years ago. It was all around.

If Nick were in a car now late at night and searched the AM dial for a faint signal from a powerful station miles and miles away, what would he find? A jock in New Orleans playing Madonna followed by Alan Jackson? Not likely. That would break format. You can't do that.

He would probably hear some raspy rant about how stupid

Obama and all the liberals are, or some guy named Carl on the phone wanting to know what the hell the Cardinals were thinking when their closer threw a curveball on a three-and-one count with two men on and their team hanging on to a one-run lead. Much of the time, a medium of imagination has been reduced to little but noise.

Fragments like these went through my mind in the days after Keillor shook our hands and went on his way. Right after he left, Irene and I joked a little about his red sneakers. What does a celebrity do if he becomes identified with always wearing red sneakers, and then one day asks himself, why am I doing this? I'm sick of them. He may decide he has to keep wearing the damn things or people will think he's off his game. A moment of absolute trivia, but if Irene and I worked in radio today we would probably be expected to ask our listeners to tweet or email their two cents on whether Keillor ought to get rid of the red sneakers. That's creative programming for you.

If Daniella heard any of the drivel about red shoes, it must have confirmed her belief that she was in the temporary care of two lunatics. We had brought her into town to see the balloons being inflated for the Thanksgiving Day parade. She saw several of them, including Santa, the Pillsbury Doughboy, and Dora, her favorite, while Grandma and Grandpa McCoy got a close look at and a few words with Garrison Keillor. Not a bad outing at all. Now I've got to get Daniella hooked on skiing so we can make that long drive home on Saturdays and turn on the radio at six p.m. before Keillor retires.

39

How Not to Run a Newsroom

If I were asked to rate my talents in a newsroom, I would say I was a pretty good editor but a lousy manager. Handling a breaking news story usually wasn't a problem. Dealing with people could be.

My conduct as a manager was peppered with too many **toos:** too sarcastic, too impatient, too obnoxious too often, too loud and boisterous, too eager to second guess, too ready to interfere, too lacking in sympathy for how difficult journalism can be and too sparing in praise when something was done really well. To my credit, I hope, I was always eager, perhaps too eager, to pitch in, writing copy or helping in a tape room when there was big news, a short staff or both.

Lacking essential social skills, I wasn't always adept either at dealing with affiliates and their concerns. During one visit to an affiliate, the news director complained that CBS Radio was terrible at giving advance notice about upcoming events that it planned to cover. AP Radio was much better, he said, reading from a series of advisories AP had sent stations.

I asked, "Did you carry any of these events?"

"No" was his answer.

Leaning toward him, I said, "Let me get this straight. You want four days advance notice of events you're not going to carry?"

The room got very still. The news director was steaming but silent. The CBS Radio affiliate representative with me finally spoke up, changing the subject. At lunch (with the snotty news director not present), the affiliate relations guy confessed that I had made a very good point.

Much has changed since I left the news business. An explosion of innovations has enabled people with sophisticated phones to capture pictures of breathtaking and, at times, revolutionary events as they happen and for those images to be seen within minutes in most parts of the world. Twitter and other social media now allow an instant exchange of opinions, and sometimes even facts, among thousands of people. As dramatic and important as these advances are, they will all probably be out-of-date in three years.

Newsrooms across America, I fear, haven't followed the world's appetite for speed. Many sound bites on radio and TV newscasts these days run on and on for five seconds or more.

Yes, I'm being sarcastic; some of us never learn. In the same vein, other excesses of modern-day journalism include:

Always trying to interview someone who likes a major new project proposed by the president of the United States or other top official. Producers and reporters do a terrible job of tracking down people who oppose various initiatives. Journalists and network bookers seem unable to locate anyone who is against anything. Strange.

Not giving nearly enough space or air time to celebrities, even minor ones, when they are caught doing bad things.

Dropping a sensational story from newscasts or newspapers the second there are no new developments. What's wrong with rehashing and rehashing endlessly?

A nasty habit of overplaying even the most trivial news out of China, India and Africa. Viewers, listeners and readers can only digest so much information, and anything that happens outside North America is really of no import to most Americans. The silly frenzy over the so-called Greek financial crisis was proof of that, if any were needed.

Spending too much time and space on identifying the financial backing and political leanings of dozens of interest groups whose spokespersons are quoted in stories.

Not nearly enough focus on medical studies involving 50 or fewer people in Sweden and Norway.

(Along about here, my editor, Irene, says I need to remind

readers again of my deep devotion to sarcasm. Consider yourself reminded.)

All too often a too grim approach to the news. Never smiling or laughing or thanking reporters on the air after their reports or chatting with them about their personal lives.

Too many in-depth pieces and articles explaining the nuts and bolts of President Obama's health care program and how it was supposed to work and paying way too little attention to the day-to-day political scrimmaging over it.

Bogging pieces down with way too much sourcing. One source should be plenty for any story. If that one source doesn't know what he or she is talking about, that's not the reporter's fault. It's up to the audience to sort things out. Reporters are much too busy to get sidetracked down this blind alley. Solid journalists never talk to several experts about a story. They find one person representing a company, industry or interest group and build their piece around that individual and then slap it on the air.

An overwhelming reluctance to tell avid consumers of media anything at all about Anderson Cooper. Where he buys his sweaters, what he uses on his hair, what his normal day is like, what he likes to eat, how much sleep he needs, what his favorite color is and so forth. It's a blind spot that's hard to explain. Frankly, it's mystifying.

But then those of us in our 70s find much of what's happening all around us these days mystifying. There's no reason the news business should be an exception. From my retirement couch on Long Island, I do, however, have some tips for current and future TOMs on what not to do when running a newsroom. If you think these are some of the no-noes I committed, you would be right.

Wind-up toys, especially those of private body parts, are fun at parties and in bars but probably don't belong on a manager's desk. If they are on the desk, then they certainly should not be wound and put into action when someone comes in to see you, especially the mothers of staff members or company vice presidents. Also when introduced to the mother of a woman staffer do not ask this courteous lady if she spent much of her time as a teenager in the back of a 1954 Dodge.

People who work for you get tired of hearing the same wise-crack every day about their tie or shirt and hearing daily lewd descriptions of what their lunch or their hair looks like. No, I don't know why. They just do.

Don't assume that most people will read the staff memos you write, even though they should. When it becomes obvious that hardly anyone has read an important memo, don't have a fit—an "outburst"—and chuck the staff memo clipboard into the waste-basket or make a dramatic display of deleting the staff memo file in the computer. If you do either, then the four people who do always read staff memos can't because they no longer exist.

Restrain yourself when you have to remind the staff, for what seems like the eight hundredth time, about newsroom policy on a sensitive issue or how to handle certain situations. Don't show your disgust by including an obtuse set of letters at the end of your memo. My favorite was ILMACYHTDITAD—it's like milking a cow, you have to do it twice a day.

Even if your organization—let's say it's the Jupiter News Service—is doing a horrible job chasing a big story do not yell at the newest desk assistant, someone who has been there all of two days, demanding, "Call Jupiter News Service and see what they're doing on this story." The kid won't understand this attempt at subtlety. Don't forget, you may end up asking him or her for a job one day.

When a young lady is wearing an extremely short and inap-propriate skirt in the newsroom, do not ask her, "How did the interview with Fox News go?"

Do not hang pictures in your office of yourself making a popular street gesture, even if the picture was given to you by someone in the company you genuinely like.

Don't keep a messy office with newspapers, books, tapes, candy wrappers, baseball hats, a bull whip, telephone books and dozens of other items—both alive and dead—scattered all over. You may hear from your boss if he sits in your office when you're on vacation, and, after finding a very soggy bag of grapes hidden under papers on your desk, he feels obligated to stroll out into the newsroom to share this discovery with the staff.

When a young writer candidate starts taking notes on what you are saying and asking questions about health benefits and how long it normally takes for people to get promoted, don't explode and leap from your chair and bellow at this poor creature that you are not running a Boy Scout camp and demand that he stop what he's doing and remove his buns from your office forthwith if not sooner.

At the start of a writer's audition do not ask the candidate if she is an idiot, and when she says, "no" jump in and reply "good. Because we already have enough idiots." Companies, big and small, across the U.S. make room for new idiots all the time. If they didn't, where would the next batch of TOMs come from?

If something goes terribly wrong close to a deadline, don't throw anything—in your office, in the newsroom or anywhere else. The throw-nothing edict includes telephones, computers, CDs, TV sets, staplers, pens, pencils, people, clipboards, wastebaskets, food, clothing, toiletries, shoes, coffee, coffee mugs, coins, reams of paper. I repeat. Throw nothing.

I suppose I should confess that it probably wouldn't have killed me to say "good morning" when greeted at the start of the day by staff members instead of my usual, surly, "It's hardly morning in any civilized part of the world." Although it may be way too late, here goes: "Good morning, good morning, good morning, good morning...."

And thanks, and good night.

P.S. No, I have no intention to apologize for rolling my eyes and shaking my head when told a writer or anchor had called in sick because his dog died.

Readers Guide

1. The author gives a one-word description of performance reviews. What would be your one-word description?
2. If editors made more money than anchors, would the copy read by anchors be better?
3. Would you like to have worked in a newsroom with Larry McCoy?
4. If you answered "no," how about if you had been allowed to carry a loaded weapon?
5. If editors made more money than anchors, would more editors use hair spray?
6. Do you think McCoy is too harsh in his treatment of TOMs, Turkeys of Management?
7. What's the worst thing a TOM ever did to you?
8. What's the nicest (or almost nice) thing you ever saw a TOM do?
9. If editors made more money than anchors, would more editors be hired solely for their looks?
10. Do you think you would have enjoyed being McCoy's boss?
11. If you answered "yes," why in the world would you say that?
12. If editors made more money than anchors, would editors engage in more small talk and laughter at their desks?
13. Now that you know a little about the author and his penchant for troublemaking do you think he could have kept a steady job in some field other than news? Before answering, keep in mind that toll booth operators in the New York City area seem to hire only surly people.
14. During the writers' strike in 1987, McCoy's wife Irene and their son Jack wanted to kill him. Was it because?

> (A) The writers' strike had nothing to do with it. They had felt that way for a long time.
>
> (B) As a manager he was working very long hours and when Irene or Jack picked him up from the train station around midnight, he insisted on eating at a diner where, every damn night, he had a

salad and a big bourbon, putting the bill on his CBS credit card.

15. The author denounces American news media for excessive coverage of the British royal family. Do you think this is one time when he's right?
16. CBS News had several presidents while McCoy was there, but he only mentions two of them, Andrew Heyward and Sean McManus. Here are three tales about other CBS News presidents that didn't make the book.

> (A) One of them began a meeting of top editors and producers by describing with great passion the body of Sandra Bullock.
> (B) Another told a meeting that CBS News had "to come down hard" on the availability of automatic weapons. After a long silence, a producer, now with "60 Minutes," suggested in a firm voice "that's not what we do." McCoy believes the idea died in that meeting.
> (C) McCoy would stop in the men's room before heading for the train home, and one night a radio technician was standing in front of a urinal as he entered. They were soon joined by the president of CBS News. After the technician finished, he walked over to the sink to wash his hands. "Joe," McCoy said, "the only reason you're washing your hands is because the president of CBS News is here." Joe laughed as did the president of CBS News. Joe left and soon afterward so did the president of CBS News, without washing his hands.

17. Of the three snippets about CBS News presidents, you liked C best, didn't you?
18. Do you feel that anyone who works in news has dirty hands?
19. If there is a Heaven, do you think they'll let any broadcast journalists in besides Edward R. Murrow and Walter Cronkite?
20. If editors made more money than anchors, would all women editors show up at work in short skirts and well-tanned legs?

Bibliography

Gelb, Arthur. *City Room.* Berkley Books, New York, 2005

Goldberg, Bernard. *Arrogance.* Warner Books, New York, 2003

Hamill, Pete. *News Is A Verb: Journalism at the End of the Twentieth Century.* The Library of Contemporary Thought, New York, 1998

index

(Note: Some of the outstanding folks I worked with are listed under "People." There is a separate listing for "Stringers And Others Heard On CBS Radio." No inference should be drawn that stringers aren't considered people.)

CPSIA information can be obtained
at www.ICGtesting.com
Printed in the USA
FFOW05n0134090115

9 781632 930415